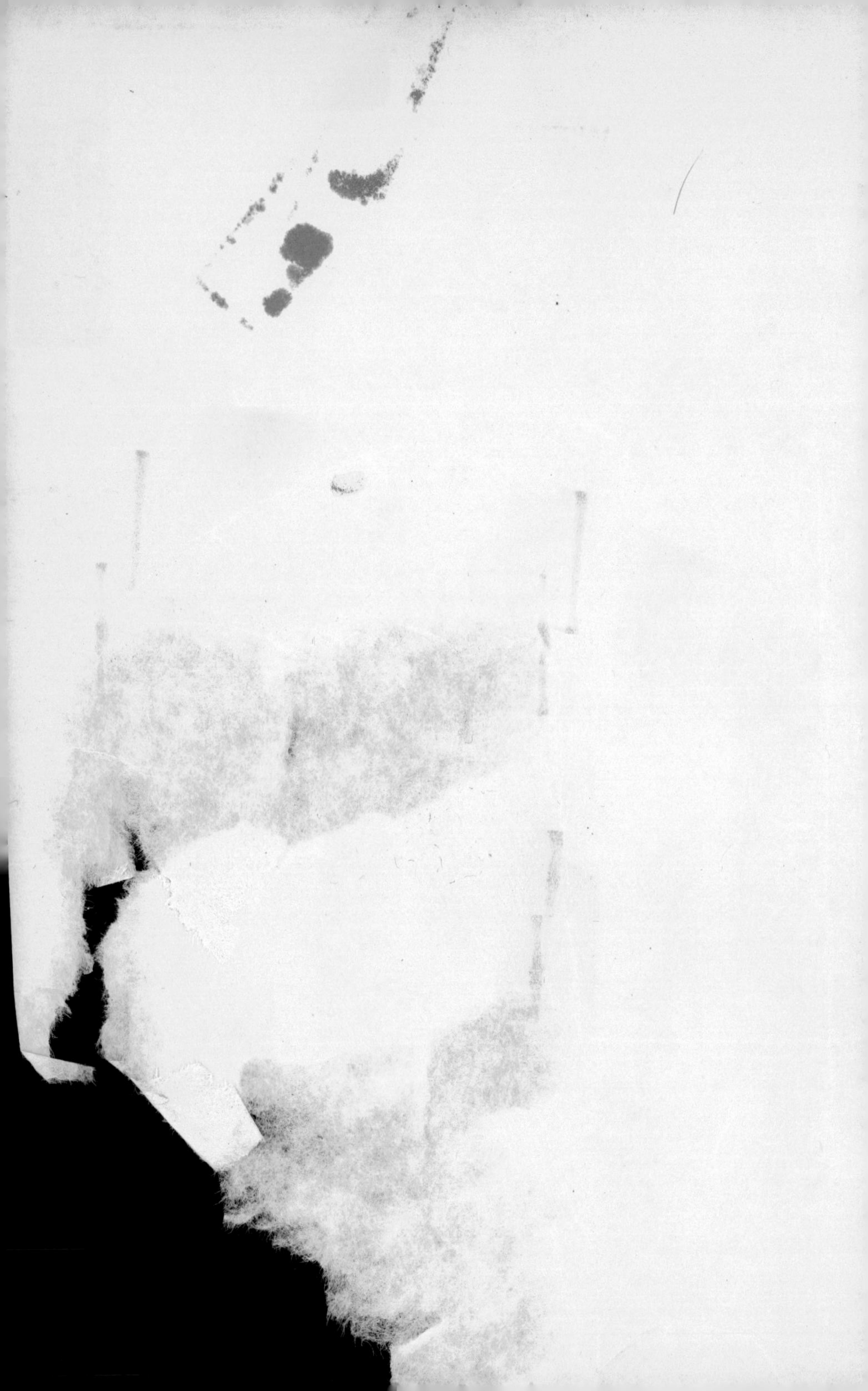

# JOHN SLOAN

*A Painter's Life*

VAN WYCK BROOKS *has written:*

MAKERS AND FINDERS: A History of the Writer in America, 1800-1915

I. The World of Washington Irving

II. The Flowering of New England

III. The Times of Melville and Whitman

IV. New England: Indian Summer

V. The Confident Years: 1885-1915

OPINIONS OF OLIVER ALLSTON

THE LIFE OF EMERSON

THE ORDEAL OF MARK TWAIN

THE PILGRIMAGE OF HENRY JAMES

EMERSON AND OTHERS

THREE ESSAYS ON AMERICA: America's Coming-of-Age, Letters and Leadership, The Literary Life in America

SKETCHES IN CRITICISM

A CHILMARK MISCELLANY

THE WRITER IN AMERICA

SCENES AND PORTRAITS: Memories of Childhood and Youth

JOHN SLOAN: A Painter's Life

Published by E. P. DUTTON & CO., INC.

JOHN SLOAN, 1939

*In his studio at the Hotel Chelsea*

# JOHN SLOAN

## *A Painter's Life*

*by*

Van Wyck Brooks

*With 25 illustrations*

E. P. DUTTON & CO., INC.
*NEW YORK* 1955

FIRST EDITION

LIBRARY OF CONGRESS CATALOG CARD NUMBER: 55-5350

To

HELEN SLOAN

*Dear Helen,*

*Ever since I began this book I have thought constantly of something you wrote to me a year ago: "I know you are going to enjoy working with the Sloan subject because it is compact and has 'presence' and never fails in human qualities."*

*How entirely right you were in saying just this! And how grateful I am to you for making this book possible by the skill and care with which you arranged John Sloan's papers. You remember the remark of his friend Glackens, "Artists say the silliest things." But art-critics say sillier things in their attempt to translate into another idiom the language of the brush. Partly because of my ignorance of the more technical questions of painting—ignorant as I also am of the art-critic's language—I have attempted only to tell a plain story, and whatever success I may have had in this endeavour of mine I owe to the "human qualities" that inhere in the subject. Thanks to your kind forethought, I have spent many happy months in the presence of your great husband who was my old friend.*

*Always yours affectionately,*

Van Wyck Brooks

*September, 1954*

For so kindly helping him with the illustrations in this book the author is most grateful to Miss Antoinette Kraushaar of the Kraushaar Galleries and Miss Rosalind Irvine of the Whitney Museum of American Art. For the frontispiece he is indebted to Goro, Black Star.

# CONTENTS

# LIST OF ILLUSTRATIONS

## CHAPTER I

# PHILADELPHIA

When John Sloan was growing up in the last quarter of the nineteenth century, "American art was,—well, it was American." So remarked a certain writer who also said that "American taste" could not be persuaded to value its own productions. The drawing-rooms of the elect were adorned with French academic and Barbizon artists, along with the "great cow painters," as Frank Crowninshield called them, while for Whistler's "Mother" no one was willing to pay even the small price that the French government paid in the middle nineties. In those days the dealers' rooms were like "funeral parlours," one artist said, "in which the cadavers were displayed in sumptuous coffins," and "art was at its lowest ebb," John Sloan himself remembered, in its "pursuit of visual imitation."

How differently, half a century later, one used the phrase "American art," with what dissimilar feelings and connotations, when everyone agreed with Sloan that the painting to which it referred was, to say the least, "healthy and exciting." There were many reasons for this change,—involved in America's coming of age,—as a result of which artists were able to dispense with what one of them called "the persistent glamour of the European scene." But one of the reasons undoubtedly was the "prompt, relentless effort," as Everett Shinn called it, of Sloan and his friends, "without which art in America would have slept on, hobbled on, sinking lower and lower into cosmetic displays." That the first really significant movement in the development of a national art sprang from this group of artists, and especially from Sloan, many writers have testified in the last two decades, whether or not the Irish painter John Butler Yeats overstated the claims of his friend in New York. What, truly or otherwise, Yeats wrote to another friend in Europe was, "England and America have produced only two serious painters, Hogarth and Sloan (not including Blake who was more poet than painter and not including landscape painters)."

Born in 1871, John Sloan was six years old when his family settled in Philadelphia. There he was to live for twenty-seven years, meeting Robert Henri there and taking his own first steps in art before he went on to New York as an etcher and painter. His birthplace was Lock Haven on the Susquehanna, a lumbering town where, as Sloan recalled, the girls were secluded in the springtime to keep them away from the loggers who swarmed in the streets. His father's forbears had been cabinet-makers and undertakers and his mother had been a school-teacher in her youth in the town. As a famous native son, Sloan was astonished in later years by the beauty of the hills and the river when he revisited the scene, for he had remembered nothing clearly but the small flight of stairs at the rear of the house,—still in good trim, he found—in which he was born.

Before they moved into the heart of the city, the Sloans had stopped in Germantown, where Joseph Pennell was living a block or two away, one of the many Philadelphia artists who left the town, first or last, preferring to live in London or New York. Thence the father of American art, Benjamin West, had gone abroad to be followed by Robert Fulton, who was born near by,—and others of the "tribe of Benjamin," West's London pupils,—to be followed again four generations later by their fellow-Pennsylvanian Mary Cassatt. It was natural enough that "no Philadelphian was ever a genius in Philadelphia," for an "instinct of disparagement" was bred in the bone there,—in the phrases of two writers who lived in the town,—and a case in point was Thomas Eakins who spent a long life, in the phrase of another, "buried under the Philadelphia mildew." Eakins met nothing all his days but apathy and antagonism in this great city where artists had always abounded, the home of the first American sculptor, the admirable William Rush, and the first American school that was devoted to art. Founded by Charles Willson Peale, the Pennsylvania Academy was still the most progressive school in the country, and Eakins's successor Thomas Anshutz, who was Henri's teacher and Sloan's for a time, gave John Marin a prize for his school drawings. As a centre of magazine publishing, Philadelphia was a focus too for artists in black and white, engravers and etchers. Pennell, Abbey and A. B. Frost had been students in Eakins's life-class, and the novelist Frank R. Stockton had begun as a wood-engraver in the town where Sloan and his circle began as newspaper artists.

John Sloan's father was a sort of artist *manqué,* one of those natural craftsmen whose work was taken out of their hands and replaced by the machine and mass-production. He was a Sherwood Anderson character in real life. Cut out for some fine handicraft, such as his father had practised, an artist and inventor in grain, he was a misfit, floundering through several occupations and ending as a defeated man, gentle, sensitive, melancholy, broken. Copying pictures in oil at night, decorating china and pottering about the house as a handyman, he walked with his head bent and his eyes on the ground. For a while he had been a travelling salesman for Marcus Ward and Company, the British manufacturers of writing paper who published delightful children's books, the illustrations of Walter Crane and the gay little greeting-cards that Sloan knew as a child. The Marcus Ward productions were strewn through the house, for Mrs. Sloan's sister, who had gone to school in Switzerland, had married the publisher's son, William H. Ward. This English uncle was to write in time an article in *The Studio* on the painting of Marianna Sloan, who was John Sloan's sister;* while

* A gifted artist, Marianna Sloan continued to paint for many years with a fair measure of professional success. She taught water-colour painting to small classes and made lampshades and screens in a semi-decorative style that was "related to Corot," as her brother put it. Her murals in St. Thomas's Episcopal church in the suburb of Whitemarsh, containing more than two hundred life-size figures, somewhat suggested John LaFarge's fresco in the Church of the Ascension in New York. With her bright mind and wit, Marianna Sloan was "what is called a 'character,'" John Sloan said. In later years she conducted a rare-book shop in Germantown.

Sloan was indebted to another uncle, his mother's uncle, Alexander Priestley,* for his first knowledge of the work of Hogarth. For this uncle who invented a method of making paper from wood-pulp owned elephant folios of Hogarth and Rowlandson prints. From his earliest boyhood, Sloan was familiar with good examples of graphic art, among them "old Tenniel's faithful classic drawings that have grown fast to the book like moss to stone," as, writing of *Alice in Wonderland,* Sloan said later; and a water-colour of Dedham Castle, supposedly original, by Turner, always hung in the Sloans' Philadelphia house. "Our Turner," as the Sloans called it, was the subject of Sloan's first etching, a "pale little plate," as he described it, in 1888.

The Sloans had very small means, and John Sloan remembered all his life the goodness and the serenity of his valiant mother. When she had passed through years of invalidism he was to commemorate her in a fine portrait-etching. While the father, Scotch-Irish by descent, was originally a Presbyterian,† the mother was an Episcopalian of the High Church order, and Sloan, who was a choir-boy for years, "tried to think of sins to talk about," he said, when he went to confes-

* The Sloans believed they were collaterally descended from the discoverer of oxygen, the English revolutionist Joseph Priestley, the friend of Jefferson who settled in America in 1794 and lived and died at Northumberland on the Susquehanna. An old engraving of Priestley hung in their house, but they seem to have had no definite proof of the connection.

† "I am Irish and agin the government," John Sloan often said; but, although some of his forbears had lived in Belfast, they were all of Scottish or English Protestant descent.

Of a Presbyterian aunt's life, Sloan said it was so narrow that it "would have been in a draught in a lemonade straw."

sion. He liked the forms and colour of the High Church ritual, the incense and the stations of the cross, which never quite lost for him their element of magic,* but, while his two sisters were, as he put it, "quite desperate" in their church-going, he gradually withdrew from the Church when he was about sixteen. Later he said, "Henri pulled my religious tooth," and he also said that Bakunin's *God and the State* "clarified some of my feeling about religion," but long before he read this he had read sympathetically Voltaire and Paine and heard various discussions of the theory of evolution. For Sloan was a great reader even as a boy, and he spent every Saturday at the public library, bringing his lunch so that he could read all day. One upshot of this was that he became a Humanist, the designation he liked in after years, convinced already, in spite of his mother, that "religiousness and goodness" were, as he expressed it, "very different things." As an older man he said that he would have joined the Humanist Society if he had been what is called a joiner, for its philosophy that "we are here to grow, slowly, more human" was just what he had worked out for himself.†

* This accounted for his remark about Bishop Fulton J. Sheen, who seemed to be making converts right and left, "I'd really be afraid to meet that man." Fearing that he would be "mesmerized," he continued, "I would feel like a wooden Indian with a termite in his pocket."

† Years later he said he found his beliefs expressed in Corliss Lamont's book, *Humanism as a Philosophy*.

Reverent by nature, Sloan always disliked religious pictures that were low in feeling. Of a certain painting of the Crucifixion he remarked, "It is a greater insult to Christ than the Christian religion."

Sloan painted only one picture with religious subject-matter, "I Must be About My Father's Business." Painted for an exhibition

As a boy, Sloan always read in preference to playing games, though he also tinkered at carpentry and liked machines, while his friend William J. Glackens at the Central High School, already a brilliant draughtsman, was a lover of baseball. Because of this taste which they shared in common, Glackens was a friend of Albert C. Barnes, who later became so famous as an art collector and who was to make a fortune through his invention of Argyrol a few years after he left the Central High School. Glackens was then to form the nucleus of the great Barnes collection, advising his friend to put in the attic the red-heads by Henner that he had acquired,—with his Millets, Diazes and Corots,—and start afresh. Barnes gave Glackens a letter of credit to take with him to Paris, whence he sent back the first Renoirs, Cézannes and Matisses that were followed by so many others at the Barnes Foundation; and, meanwhile, Barnes bought two of his schoolmate John Sloan's paintings, one of them the first painting that Sloan ever sold.

At sixteen, Sloan himself, obliged to earn his living, had gone to work in the bookstore of Porter and Coates, an easy-going old-fashioned establishment where he was assistant cashier and had ample time to browse over the books. He ran through sets of Balzac and Zola, Victor Hugo and Maupassant, discovering the "gloriously jolly" Rabelais with the

---

of pictures with the theme of the childhood of Christ, arranged by Marie Sterner, this, far from being a typical Sloan, was an anomaly in his work, like his Treasury Department mural.

Towards the end of his life, Sloan attempted, with similar ill success, a picture with a mythological subject, "Tyro and Poseidon." One might say that, in general, he was only happy in representing subjects that he had seen.

illustrations of Gustave Doré who remained one of his heroes as a draughtsman in black and white. He was drawn to the robust erotic humour of the French story-tellers, disliking the artificial and the morbidly romantic; but, what was more important for him, he browsed as well in the print department over the original etchings of Rembrandt and Dürer. The head of the department helped him to make pen-and-ink copies of Rembrandt prints,—of the artist, especially, leaning on the window-sill,—that were sold in the store for five or ten dollars; and, reading Hamerton's *Etcher's Handbook* and obtaining a plate, a needle and a roller, Sloan taught himself how to etch. He went on from "our Turner" to heads of English authors. Among these were George Eliot and Ruskin, and he also etched for calendars a series of "Homes of American Poets" and another series from photographs of Westminster Abbey. Then A. Edward Newton, later the well-known bibliophile, set up a "fancy goods" business and asked Sloan to join him; for Newton, who had been a clerk in the stationery department of Porter and Coates, liked his drawings for valentines and the jingles that went with them. At Newton's Sloan designed Christmas cards, match-boxes and book-marks, while there were twenty-eight girls in the shop decorating novelties and painting candy-boxes with French lovers flirting on the lids. Newton supervised the packing of these hand-painted boxes which were sent on to Maillard's and Huyler's in New York. With his prominent china-blue eyes, he would emerge from the basement, holding out a box that had been blemished, saying to the most skilful of the painters, "There is a spot on the box, Miss Lawrence. Will you drop a violet on it?" Miss

Lawrence, the life of the painting-room, twisted her brush into three or four colours and forthwith adroitly dropped the blossom.

As the only young man among twenty-eight girls, John Sloan was not too happy, for they made merry over him, knowing that he was afraid of them, and the more fearful he was the more they teased him. Later he said he was "deathly afraid of women and their wiles" and thought they were put into the world to keep artists from working, explaining that he always played the clown at parties as a form of self-defence when girls were around. He made jokes and took part in skits and pantomimes so that he would not have to talk with them. He wished above all to be free of domestic entanglements, and it was partly this fear of girls that kept him from going to Paris when so many of his friends who were art students were going. A. Edward Newton asked Sloan to go abroad with him, although he withdrew the invitation later, but for a number of reasons of which this was only one Sloan did not really wish to go. He took it for granted that having a mistress and "piling up saucers in a café" were necessary ingredients of a student's life in Paris, but a deeper reason behind this,—a paradox indeed,—was that, in a sense, he was not interested in art. At least one can fairly say that in his twenties and early thirties only graphic art concerned him profoundly, and when he was twenty-two he said that he did not "expect to be an artist" and felt he was "a newspaper man painting on the side." * For the rest,

* Sloan had begun to draw very early. He had illustrated his own copy of *Treasure Island,* the book he liked best as a boy.

He also copied in a notebook "all the illustrations," as he said, "in the dictionary."

he was reading at this time George Moore's *Modern Painting,* which made, he observed, a strong impression on him, a book that rather stressed the "injurious effect" that travel often had on art and artists. It was a well-known fact that Rembrandt refused to leave home when people said he should go to Italy and study the old masters in that wonderful land, remarking that, while it was good for a few, he could learn his trade in Holland and that going to Italy for him would be a waste of time. He felt, moreover, that artists living in Holland should get their emotions from subjects which they knew well and not from something a thousand miles away; and George Moore said that the desire for travel had destroyed Dutch art at its greatest moment. Advising artists to stay at home, George Moore also said that all the great modern artists were self-educated men, that Whistler, Degas, Courbet, Corot and Manet had "wasted little time" in the studios of others. (Scarcely true, of course, but let that pass.) Paul Potter had learned his trade in the fields, Old Crome, the English landscapist, had been a house-painter, and Moore asked if Morland would have done better work if he had spent three or four years studying at South Kensington from the antique.

One can imagine John Sloan pondering these questions, finding reasons for agreeing with Moore in part because his views were in certain ways harmonious with Robert Henri's. Sloan's own master in days to come was all for what he called "life, not art," while, studying in Europe himself, he had ignored the old masters,—or all but two or three who appealed to him,—and Henri seemed to corroborate Emerson who said one should work from the familiar scenes of home. Moore also despised academies and their commonplace ideals, and he wrote in praise of the Japanese prints that Sloan was discovering for himself and extolled Charles Keene as a great artist. Keene, he said, was "content to tell the story of his own country and the age he lived in" while he "worked as did the Dutchmen of 1630," all of which must have impressed Sloan, who was steeping himself in Keene and Leech, the English black-and-white artists who had drawn for *Punch*. Sloan, whose only conscious ambition was to be an illustrator, felt that for this reason an art school would have been his undoing,—though he went to two art schools, briefly, nevertheless; and, as for going abroad, Eakins's views on that subject must have been long familiar to him. For Eakins, to Sloan, was "the greatest American painter, the only great American painter who has yet occurred," and Eakins had come to feel that going abroad was no longer important as it had been when he was a young art student.*

In years to come Sloan changed his mind about many questions of life and art when the Armory Show and the

* "If America is to produce great painters and if young art students wish to assume a place in the history of art in this country, their first desire should be to remain in America, to peer deeper into the heart of American life, rather than to spend their time abroad obtaining a superficial view of the art of the old world. In the days when I studied abroad conditions were entirely different. The facilities for study in this country were meagre . . . Far better for American art students and painters to study their own country and to portray its life and types . . . Americans must . . . strike out for themselves, and only by doing this will we create a great and distinctly American art."—Quoted in Lloyd Goodrich's *Thomas Eakins*.

While Eakins made these statements in an interview in 1914, it may be assumed that he had held for many years the views in question.

"ultra-modern" movement had rapidly aroused his interest in the old masters, convinced as he was that the new painters had revived for all to see "the old, the permanent, the universal principles" of art. He regretted after this that he had not gone abroad, for it would have meant much to him to see more of the old masters, but if he felt this occasionally only it was in large part because so many of the old masters had been brought to this country. He was able to see many of them in New York.* In the meantime he had become absorbed in the life about him, as Mount and Winslow Homer had been absorbed before him, and all the Dutch genre painters earlier still; and that this gave him a certain advantage one saw by considering the work of his friends who had gone to France only to be overborne there. Later he wrote, "You can't show American painters in Paris without hearing their critics point out what the French derivations were, and therefore pass the work by." He might have been referring to Everett Shinn, whose artistic personality was a compound of Degas, Fragonard, Boucher and Watteau, or to his older friend Glackens whose work was indistinguishable, or almost so, at times, from Manet's or Renoir's. For one reason or another, Sloan was always Sloan, and incidentally American, never French; and the result was, as Walter Pach observed, that the French critics especially signalized him. In general, "Europeans, visiting New York, have always been struck by Sloan," said Pach in an article in the

* Even in his youth he had seen a good many in Philadelphia. He visited the Widener collection once, but he saw a number of times the John G. Johnson collection. There, he wrote later, "even the doors were hung with pictures on both sides. I like to go into the home of a collector who really enjoys living with pictures."

*Virginia Quarterly Review,* partly because, after all the tiresome vague reminiscences of Europe, his work seemed to them peculiarly transatlantic. One found there no Italian peasants, Dutch windmills or Paris streets, and on several occasions French writers have chosen Sloan, Pach went on, as "the most significant American painter today." This was a compensation for what he may have lost by failing to study abroad or travel there.

But,—not to look too far ahead,—although Sloan seemed indifferent to study, he went to evening art-classes when he was at Newton's, at first at the Spring Garden Institute, a Philadelphia Cooper Union where Everett Shinn was a student of mechanical drawing. Then he went on to the Pennsylvania Academy to work with Thomas Anshutz, Eakins's disciple, who carried on there the precepts of his master and who had a similar sober brush and never looked abroad for his ideas or his subjects. The dark dank old Academy building was a byword among artists for whom it "yawned like a tomb," as one of them said,—a "fusty fudgy place" with the trail all over it of "dismal persons who thought themselves old masters." There hung West's "Death on a Pale Horse" and other "grand" paintings, with portraits by Gilbert Stuart, Sully and the Peales, heirlooms of the city's intellectual past that were intermingled with the work of a few living academic painters. Thomas Eakins had been dethroned for posing male and female models together to show the differences in their structure, and once when the model failed to arrive he had asked one of the girls in the class to take off her clothes and get up on the model stand. He regarded draperies as a concession to low ideas,—which did not please the

Philadelphians,—for this great teacher was obsessed with anatomy and would take home a forearm or a leg in order to cut it up of a winter evening. Liking, he said, to construct his men so that they would be "solid and springy and strong," Eakins had been one of the first of his generation to see Velasquez in his native Spain, and, hating what he called affectation, he loved in the Spaniards the breath of reality after the artificiality of the Salons. Grave and reserved, he was often taken for a Spaniard himself, while, with his feeling for mass and for balance and with his powerful browns and greys, he had no more gaiety or lightness than the humourless Anshutz. The taste of his time was for darkness in both pictures and houses.

All his life John Sloan revered Thomas Eakins, who loved his native world as Sloan did also, the friend of Walt Whitman who was likewise at home, deeply at home, in America, in spite of all he suffered from neglect there. Eakins, ignored and rebuffed, withdrawing from the world, ended by painting relatives and friends to whom he presented the portraits they were sometimes too indifferent to carry away, —portraits that were "more the artist than the sitter," Sloan said, adding that Eakins "never let his eye run away with his brain." He had seldom, except in irony, spoken of "beauty," and in this John Sloan was to follow him for years, while Sloan shared Eakins's love of solidity and dark colours too, although he derived this taste more directly from Henri. But, having no contact with Eakins himself, Sloan only received the master's ideas through the intermediation of Thomas Anshutz, deep-seated ideas about getting substance and reality in their work which the disciple in turn passed on to his pupils. Modelling muscles in clay himself and fixing them on the skeleton, analyzing the figure with its major solids, urging them to study the texture of things, he was the teacher not only of Sloan but of Henri, Glackens, Shinn and Edward Redfield. Or, rather, in Sloan's case, he would have been the teacher if Sloan himself had been seriously ready for him. Years later, when Anshutz died, Sloan praised his "splendid manly service," but as a young man at the Academy he had fallen out with Anshutz, when, at the end of his second term, the teacher had rebuked him because he was bored with anatomy and drawing from casts. Sloan, who had pulled his chair over to the wall, was sketching some of the other students, for he was much more interested in the life about him; and, leaving the class that day, he never went back.

CHAPTER II

# HENRI AND HIS CIRCLE

JOHN SLOAN was twenty-one years old when he first met Robert Henri, "my father in art," as he later wrote, "up to the time of the Armory Show," who "kept after me to think of being a serious painter." Sloan had become a newspaper artist, working for the *Inquirer,*—he had wandered one day into the art department while he was still at A. Edward Newton's,—drawing decorative headings for the Sunday edition and illustrations chiefly for the women's section. He had already seen much of Henri when three years later he joined the *Press* and the "old stock company" that was more or less connected with it. This was Henri's phrase for his younger associates who were all newspaper artists, Glackens, George Luks, James Preston and Everett Shinn, "the 'kid' of our crowd," as John Sloan called him, who was not actually on the staff, while Glackens had gone to New York when Sloan joined the paper. But Sloan's old friend Glackens, like Shinn, had been one of the circle, and with Edward Davis, the art director,—the father of Stuart Davis, the abstractionist, later,—they formed a lively group in the office and outside. Henri, perceiving their talents at once, had urged them to paint as well as draw, and, though Sloan was not Henri's pupil in the technical sense, it was Henri who aroused his wish to be a painter. Sloan was closer to this born teacher, who was six years older than himself,—"the old man," as they all called him,—than any of the others; and, for Henri, Sloan was a sort of younger brother.

A great teacher, beyond a doubt, whose pupils were to include in time many of the best young artists also in New York,—when he established his school in the Lincoln Arcade there,—Henri had emerged in Philadelphia out of a Bret Harte story of the West, where his father, a land-speculator, was also a professional gambler. Henri's actual original name had been Robert Henry Cozad, and, dropping the patronymic, he had altered the Henry, while his father, after whom the town of Cozad, Nebraska, was named, now lived at Atlantic City under the name of Lee. He had become there a prosperous real-estate broker, and his melodramatic Far Western past, as a faro-player who had killed his man and fled from the scene with his wife, was buried and forgotten. During the old cattle-grazing days, he had killed this man in self-defence and he had been acquitted in a trial; but he still went to Saratoga, when the family funds were low, to "clean up" at the gambling tables there. Henri made no secret of this,—in fact, he was rather proud of it; but one might have found here a reason for his reserve, for no one felt really intimate with him and he had an air of mystery that Sloan felt he liked to cultivate because it added to his prestige. In the late eighties, after studying with Anshutz, he had gone to Paris, where he spent eleven years off and on,—a student both at Julien's and the Beaux-Arts,—and the French government had bought one of his pictures for the Luxembourg when he was still unrecognized at home. Those were the great days in France when the modern movement was taking shape with Renoir, Cézanne, Van Gogh, Gauguin and others, but Henri never had any interest either in Impressionism or in the new moderns except Rouault and a few Cézannes. He loved the spontaneous "immediate" work of Frans Hals, Goya and Velasquez and could see no vitality in a picture unless it showed on the surface, and he was interested in technique only as a means of expressing the livingness and movement of things. He was "blind," Sloan said later, "to the intellectual substance of art" and "making pictures from life" was his great message. It was a limited message, no doubt, but stirring at a time of pale, anæmic, derivative, eclectic academics.

Sloan himself in later years drew far away from Henri and his cult of visual appearance and the surfaces of things, the beauty of easy brush-work, the impression of the moment. His interest, Sloan wrote, was for "emotional work,"—the intellectual meant nothing to him; he liked work that showed how the artist did it, in which the execution revealed the excitement of the moment; but when art was so much a matter of studio concoctions, Henri was a great emancipator. Travelling back and forth, in the nineties, between Paris and Philadelphia, he aroused in his disciples a militant desire not only to paint but to fight for their ideas and beliefs, and his injunction to "forget about art and paint pictures of what interests you in life" was like fresh air in the close studio atmosphere. He had learned in France "to see men as men instead of puppets," another of Henri's pupils once remarked, and, despising preciosities and tasteful arrangements, the pretty and the fanciful, he opened the eyes of his pupils to the world around them.* Divining the special qualities of each, he urged them to paint with real feeling, avoiding the sentimental as they eschewed the clever, disregarding, despising success, for, as he said, contemporary success almost always meant ultimate failure. Quick to recognize their gifts and generously appreciative, he was rather domineering, assuming that he was the law, repelling those who refused his domination; for he was an aggressive personality whose views regarding both life and art focussed the natural tendencies of these young men. A philosophical anarchist, a great reader of Bakunin, he influenced their ideas on social questions, discussing Henry George and Bellamy, and especially Emerson and Whitman, to whom Sloan was deeply drawn already. Henri was probably the first teacher to recognize and praise the peculiarly American integrity of Eakins and Ryder.

In days to come, for a decade or more, Henri was to be recognized as the most potent force behind the movement that freed American art from academic control, as he organized new exhibitions, discovered new talents and fought for the right of all to have a hearing. His ideas were like "yeast," Sloan said, "passed from one group to another"; and certain critics presently affirmed that if there was an American school Henri was to be described as the founder of it. Meanwhile, exciting his pupils to paint in Philadelphia, he spread the belief that all subjects are fitting for art and that the workers and their life are perhaps more fitting than

* "Henri could make anyone want to be an artist, and in his presence he could make pupils with mere flickerings of talent blossom and do work with considerable vitality."—One of John Sloan's notes.

anything else because they are closer to reality, as Tolstoy taught. Sloan, who shared for a while his studio at 806 Walnut Street, might well have spoken for them all when he said later, "I don't think I would have been a painter if I had not come under his direction"; for Henri, the "oracle" and the "obstetrician," communicated to the whole group the impulse to work at painting in their spare time. They were never to think of "beauty" or to use small brushes. Deprecating Impressionism, he denounced especially the American kind with its high key and its prettiness of blues, violets and pinks, painting himself with the dark palette that Eakins and Anshutz had used and that his pupils were to use, for a time, as well. Here Henri was all for Rembrandt and for Daumier also. He urged his pupils to paint the life they knew so well as newspaper men, though not in the tight and finished fashion that had characterized Mount and the early Eastman Johnson, for, painting himself "at white heat, controlled," as Sloan put it later, he was always praising spontaneity, immediacy, speed. He had extreme facility while Sloan had none at all. Henri had a way of discarding his canvases and making fresh starts, but Sloan stubbornly fought his canvas through. Henri said "Sloan" was "the past participle of 'Slow.' "

For, sharing Henri's studio, although he continued to live at home and spent a good part of the day at the newspaper office, Sloan had begun to paint seriously under Henri's direction, more or less, while the rest of the "stock company" were virtually Henri's pupils. At "806," which soon became, as Sloan was to recall it, "a home for homeless and indigent artists of the press," Henri lived, sleeping on a cot which they all called "the rag-bag" because of the tapestries and draperies that were tossed upon it. Henri used these hangings as backgrounds for portraits, and once a week, on Thursday evenings, when he was in Philadelphia, he criticized the work of his pupils and talked to them. One of the subjects of these informal lectures was "What it means to be an artist," and Henri presented an artist's life as a virile occupation that was fit for the "commanding" and the "energetic." He had no use for the bloodless dilettante, while he was all for artists who were bent on observing the common life in saloons, in slums, along the river. In some ways he followed the teaching technique of William Morris Hunt, a copy of whose *Talks on Art* he gave to Sloan, who was influenced in turn by Hunt when he began to teach twenty years later at the Art Students' League. There was a brief interval when Sloan and his friends had borrowed a photographer's studio and started what they called the Charcoal Club, a sketch class, a rival of the Academy's classes, at which for the first time Sloan worked from a model. Henri had dropped in and criticized the work there. But this had broken up at the end of four months, and the Academy had been happy to acquire the lamps and the studio accessories which the class had used.

These, Sloan said later, were "my college days, all the fun and no examinations," days that were partly spent on the *Press,* and with Henri partly, or with the old stock company outside the office. Sometimes on Sundays, with Glackens and others, Sloan took a trolley into the country and walked for miles "looking for a subject,"—"looking for a piece of nature," as he recalled this time, "that looked like someone else's picture." Their object on these jaunts was to paint water-colours. In the art-department of the paper, meanwhile, a dusty room with windows and walls that were plastered with caricatures of their friends and themselves, Sloan and the others "went to school," as one of them said afterwards, a school that "trained memory and quick perception." For in those days they had no camera to help them. Sloan remembered the old chairs and tables pulled close together over a floor where "Democrats" were crawling in every direction,—the common name for cockroaches in this Republican stronghold,—and the wobbling, ink-stained drawing-boards that Everett Shinn described in a perhaps too fanciful account of the scene. They drew on envelopes, menu cards, old bills, laundry checks, although Sloan himself carried a small pad in his pocket, and the city editor would appear and shout, "Who's loafing? Hi, you, George Luks, get goin'!" Luks would answer, "What yard, Massa Legree?" Perhaps it was an affair of burning freight-cars in a strike-breakers' riot, and Luks would continue, "Massa Legree, ye mout own dis ol' body but ma soul belongs to Gawd"; then, imitating a three-instrument band with a final toot on the piccolo, Luks would caper through the room and leap downstairs. Someone would ask the art-director, "How many tentacles does an octopus have?"—for he was obliged to draw the octopus of municipal graft and there were twenty departments that it had to strangle. Or the cry would be "Where's Glackens?"—who was off at a launching at Cramp's Shipyard, while Shinn was drawing a jewelry shop that had been blown up when a suicide struck a match in a gas-filled kitchen. At the moment Sloan was at the morgue, drawing the body of a

JOHN SLOAN WITH HIS FATHER AND MOTHER.

IN THE STUDIO AT 806 WALNUT ST.

MOTHER, 1906

MEMORY, 1906

suicide, a Japanese spy,—or so, at least, Shinn averred in the catalogue of an exhibition when all these men had been long since veteran artists. Sloan rarely did reportorial drawings, for he did not work with sufficient speed, and he felt he was fortunate in falling in with editors who encouraged him to work slowly and carefully on drawings "out of his head." But he told the story of one of his few assignments. He had been sent with a reporter to cover a rescue on the New Jersey coast, and the two had slept together in an abandoned coast-guard house and awakened with the snow banked all about them. It filled the room and even their shoes and clothes.

Everett Shinn was a New Jersey boy who had come to Philadelphia with an interest in engineering rather than art. He had spent a whole summer working on a tin model of a submarine, and even after he had taken up art at the Pennsylvania Academy his mind was constantly busy with mechanical devices. But Shinn, the youngster of the group, was surprisingly gifted in several ways and one saw in him already not only the painter of the future but the illustrator, writer and designer of stage-sets. A dandy who spent most of his income on clothes, gay shirts and exotic coats, he was interested in the theatre most of all, and he was ready for the influence of Degas who was to sharpen his observation of the circus and the stage in his own country. As a decorator of theatres later, he was also to write vaudeville skits as well as burlesque melodramas like *The Prune-Hater's Daughter,* and he was always ready now for the plays that Henri and his friends got up in the studio at 806 Walnut Street. One of these was *The Poison Gum-Drop,* or *The*

*Apple-Woman's Revenge,* with Glackens, Luks, Shinn and John Sloan in the cast; another was a burlesque Irish play *The Widow Cloonan's Curse,* while the acme of them all was *Twillbe.* This was a parody of George Du Maurier's book which was under attack at the moment by Anthony Comstock. All the artists were talking about *Trilby,* with Whistler's assault on the art-world and the rise of Sargent. *Twillbe* was given in a room at the Academy with Henri as Svengali and John Sloan himself in the leading part, for he was always the heroine in these burlesques. With a costume that was made by his sister Marianna, he wore huge false feet and a Burne-Jones wig.

In this play Shinn also appeared with all the others except George Luks, although Luks himself was a born entertainer, and often at their parties he was a one-man vaudeville show, stripped to the waist perhaps in a mock prize-fight. Or, stirring a Welsh rarebit for which the others were lined up waiting to be served, he would pretend to be a football quarterback calling out number-combinations with sundry asides. A Pennsylvanian, like Glackens and Sloan, the son of a doctor at Williamsport, Luks seldom appeared on Henri's evenings, and he came under Henri's influence mostly through the others, though Sloan said he sometimes claimed to have started them all. He had studied painting in Munich but had given it up for illustrating, and Sloan felt he had only returned to painting because the others seemed to enjoy it so much; but they all loved this mountebank who played the mouth-organ and sang his own praises when he was in his prime as a raconteur and actor. Besides Fielding, his favourite reading was *The Ingoldsby Legends,* and Sloan said that Baron Munchausen had really become part of him and taken on reality in his mind. He would relate how he had just licked Whitey Lewis or Bob Fitzsimmons, for it pleased him to pose as a pugilist himself, and he would amuse the crowd for hours in a saloon on Chestnut Street acting the role of a great stock-promoter, senator or banker.* Then, telling tales about his deals, he would make some nasty remark at the bar to start a rumpus while he slipped away and watched from a carefully selected vantage-point; for Luks could be vicious when he drank too much. Convinced that an artist should "see life," he had long spells of abstinence before he broke loose again to reappear with a black eye and a strange hat, saying that tramping was the only life and that he was a natural hobo who was unlucky enough to have a home. His facility and his vitality were all but superhuman. He virtually filled a copy of *Toilers of the Sea* with galloping polo ponies at an international meet.

Others of the circle were E. W. Redfield, the landscape-painter of the future, and the sculptor A. Stirling Calder, the son of another Philadelphia sculptor and later the father of a third, the inventor of the mobile, Alexander Calder. At this time Redfield was "a horticulturist, pessimist, painter and poker-fiend," John Sloan observed in one of his letters,†

* "His rumbling advance along a bar rail," Everett Shinn wrote, "was like a tank rolling on with a smiling child at the wheel and all guns popping cork. He would turn away and blow a concert blast from the corner of his mouth and dance across the floor singing, 'While strolling through the wax flower exhibition, I chanced to meet a lady fair,' etc."

† Redfield and Sloan soon drifted apart. But they met again, after forty-two years, when Redfield was seventy-seven and had, Sloan noted, eleven grandchildren. "We had," Sloan said, "a good friendly reminiscent talk."

while for Calder sculpture was "an imperative duty," as he remarked once,* and even the most needed of the arts. For he felt that in our hurly-burly world we should build "new shrines of sculptured calm" to keep "the ultimate simplicity of life in view," and he regretted that sculpture had developed in America along lines of refinement rather than of power. He remembered the master's advice in Eakins's life-class, "Attack all your difficulties at once." Sloan, who saw little of Redfield later, kept up his friendship with Calder, whose son "Sandy" was to be one of his own pupils, and meanwhile, in 1895, he wrote to Henri, who had returned to Paris, about the turbulent evenings at "806." They were having Tuesday nights now and the "noise below," he said, suggested "a herd of cattle being driven upstairs," a herd that turned out to be Shinn, Edward Davis and Redfield who were presently absorbed in a game of poker. Then in the frying-pan over the gas-jet the cheese began to simmer, for Luks, brewing punch, was making another rarebit, and the orchestra tuned up, Luks on the conch-horn, James Preston with a broken guitar and Shinn with two tin plates for cymbals. Davis played the ocarina while, for a bass-viol, Sloan scraped an easel with an umbrella. A hula-hula dance began and, donning a wig and a ballet-skirt, Sloan presently executed a *danse du ventre,* and Luks imitated every known man, beast and fiend. But Sloan wished to tell Henri too about the Swedish exhibition they were having at the Academy in Broad Street where he found Zorn's work clever but thin, too damnably clever, in fact, so clever that it lacked dignity, as he put it. "The work," Sloan wrote, "looks too easy

* See A. Stirling Calder's *Thoughts.*

for him. Where work is so easily done, thought should be harder, it seems to me." For the rest, he asked if he could not be Henri's American agent if Henri had something to send that he wished to exhibit. For a few weeks Henri had been in Holland,—"the paradise of wine, cigars and Rembrandts,"—but he had returned to Paris where Glackens had joined him. Sloan sent Christmas greetings to them both from Shinn, George Luks and himself.

In time, as members of the "Eight," these artists were to play large roles, but this was after they had all moved over to New York; and, meanwhile, as newspaper illustrators, they had witnessed scenes that appeared in one way or another in their paintings later. Luks had grown up in the mining region and Pennsylvanian miners were to figure largely in his work, while Shinn had been sent there to cover a cave-in halfway down a mine-shaft and draw the desperate efforts of the rescue squad. Disliking the bulge of copy-paper that marred the outline of a new spring suit, he had thrown the paper away and used the white satin lining of the straw hat of one of the reporters. Glackens had made drawings of the Baldwin Locomotive Works, and Shinn remembered that one glance had left on his retina the lathes, the drills, the castings, the girders and the cranes. He knew nothing whatever of the functions of any of these objects, but they were all drawn so accurately that Glackens might have been working, laboriously, for hours, from photographs. Similarly, he drew buildings, bridges and the spars, tackle and masts of ships, swiftly caught but rigged for a sailor's eye. In Sloan's opinion, Glackens was "the greatest draughtman who lived on this side of the ocean."

Sloan himself was the last of the group to leave Philadelphia, where he was to remain, in fact, until 1904; and, as he said once, "Time is longer when you are young because you are anxious to have it pass."

## CHAPTER III

# AN ILLUSTRATOR'S LIFE

BEFORE HE MET HENRI, Sloan himself had scarcely ever painted. He had only attempted a few water-colour landscapes and a few oil sketches, along with a self-portrait he had executed in 1888 on a fragment of a canvas window-shade. This was a plain earnest piece of work, he said, the work of a "plodder" with none of Henri's brilliance. He was an illustrator and continued to be one, working for the Philadelphia *Press,* drawing street-car advertisements and contributing to various magazines. He had had a card printed informing the public that he was a designer who did lettering and advertising sketches. At the same time he went on with his own etching. He made a plate of the Schuylkill river in 1894, with Glackens beside him, Sloan remembered, "absorbing his first and only lesson in etching." Sloan also remembered that, as a draughtsman, Glackens set the pace for the newspaper work of all the others.*

The nineties were peculiarly a time of "little magazines," —cousins, once removed, of the *Yellow Book* in London,—

* "Sometimes Glackens made the same drawing over fifty times. I've gone in to see him and found him surrounded by drawings that he had discarded because they weren't good enough, quite what he wanted. It would make me feel very humble. I am more apt to try to push through on the original drawing."—John Sloan, *Gist of Art.*

most of them arty and singularly coy, embarrassingly precious and crude by turns and "issued about the fifteenth of each month." In some of them "John-a-Dreams" spoke, in another "Friend Satan," for an amateur diabolism was one of their notes, with an infantilism plus decadence that went in for the exotic, together with ragged edges and olde Englysshe type. Attempting to revive the neglected arts of lettering and printing, they treated advertisements decoratively with enamelled inserts, going in also for poster work with drawings by Howard Pyle and the "pioneer" poster artist Edward Penfield. Several of the good young artists contributed to these magazines and Sloan was represented in half a dozen, among them *Gil Blas,* which appeared in Philadelphia, and the *Red Letter,* published in Boston. Others with drawings or covers by Sloan were *Bradley, His Book,* the organ of Will Bradley, who specialized in posters, *Moods,* which contained drawings also by Henri and Glackens, and the *Chap Book* of Chicago. The editor of this magazine referred to Sloan's illustrations as "good examples of age-end art," and in 1896 Sloan published in it a letter attacking the "Vitascope" because it reproduced so much that was vulgar. "The ever-recurring outrage to decency and good taste which I see in books and on the stage force me," he wrote, "into the role of Jack the Giant-Killer." He added, "I have my hammer out most of the time." Sloan once said that the first photograph taken of him showed that he was an "indignant baby," and his hammer was to be out all his life long.

Sloan was already conspicuous in what was called the poster movement before he had seen Beardsley, Steinlen or

Toulouse-Lautrec. Sometimes his work showed the influence of Walter Crane,* but oftener he followed the Japanese manner that he had picked up in 1893. At that time the Japanese art commissioner to the Chicago World's Fair had spent some time in Philadelphia, and Sloan, impressed by his sketch-book, had begun to draw himself in a flat Japanese style in black, white and grey. He worked with brush and ink, reproducing more or less the mode of the Japanese prints with which he was familiar, somewhat in the manner of Mary Cassatt—"a great figure in art," as Sloan called her later,—who was making similar colour-prints at about the same time.† He had for a while a Beardsley touch, though the strongest influence on his work continued to be that of the English Keene and Leech, and it was Henri who introduced him to the lithographs of Daumier, Forain's drawings and Goya's aquatints. For Henri, who was always thinking of something to please him, sent Sloan pictures from Paris or brought them with him when he returned to Philadelphia, saying of Daumier that he was great as a painter as well as a draughtsman and speaking of his picture, the "Third-Class Railway Carriage." "Most masterfully painted," this, said Henri. "None of the modern so highly esteemed clever smartness—but great solid simple painting." The Daumier lithographs gave Sloan the feeling of a "tonic." Writing to Henri, he went on, "I picked up a lot of back

* One of Sloan's poster drawings in the manner of Walter Crane was marked by an especially intricate textural penwork. It had a skirt covered with wriggling lines that spelled out a ribald characterization of the owner of the newspaper with which he was connected.

† In 1894, the Chicago *Inland Printer* published an article on Sloan's "Japanese" work.

numbers of *Punch* the other day full of good things by Charles Keene and Du Maurier, done before the present style of patent leather pen work became the thing." But Rembrandt, in his drawings, for Sloan, was "the wizard of them all. A Rembrandt," he wrote, "has all the dash of the cheapest illustrator—but hidden in that great style. He was the antecedent of Daumier in the study of light—simplicity —sureness."

This was in 1898 when Henri was in Paris and their friend James Preston was also there. Glackens, who had been there before, was planning to return the following year, and Henri wrote to Sloan, "You had better arrange matters to come along with him," for, as he added, "You are sorely needed." Glackens, with George Luks, had gone, as staff-artists, to Cuba for the summer months of the Spanish-American war when Sherwood Anderson and Carl Sandburg were serving in the ranks and Stephen Crane was one of the correspondents. "I can imagine Glack," Henri wrote, "kicking for more hard tack and objecting to bullets riddling his paper as he sketches,"—the bullets that pelted George Luks's train when he dived under the seat, exclaiming, with unusual candour, "I've got a future." On other occasions Luks averred that he had carried important papers out of Havana disguised as a dog, holding the packet in his mouth, though he also barked. Henri had bought the October *McClure's* and liked Glackens's sketches "immensely . . . Fine feeling in all the lines," he said, "and they give a fine feeling of how men felt down there." That deep ties bound the whole group together Sloan showed a year or two later when he wrote to Henri, who was still in Paris, and when so many of the others had settled in New York while Sloan remained in Philadelphia, "Oh, what a fine show the old comrades are making in the world and will make. Glackens of whom you say you hear but little is doing work which I am sure you see and admire. Shinn, settled down and togged up, is the pet of a certain theatrical clique in New York—runs around in morning, afternoon and evening clothes with hats from the stiff silks to the sorts that are most in their element when you sit on them. Calder whose work in the exhibition this year is of a kind which I see much more good in than most modern sculpture . . . Reddy [Redfield] too. There is a stunning thing of his at the Academy now. Water in front, trees and buildings in background, sunlight breaking through and striking on top of the buildings. Perhaps you have seen it as it was done abroad. He has a couple of others which are bang up." By this time Sloan could already look back on what he described years later as "the wonderful evenings of our past at 806." Shinn had been the first to go to New York, and it was his reports that attracted the others.

Henri, in the meantime, was troubled about Sloan partly because a girl was pursuing him, a rather aggressive girl who had been sending him letters and poems ever since his performance in the burlesque *Twillbe*. At last she had written to Henri, who was anxious on Sloan's account, fearing he might be entangled with the wrong person and urging his friend to join him in Paris because, as he said, "Your success and happiness mean a great deal to me." Henri added, "Of course I am not so much worried about your taking a mistress and all that—most men do more or less—and a good many come out of it all right . . . Well, don't forget that you are John Sloan and don't give up the old studio ideas. For you are no ordinary man." He was convinced, for the rest, that Sloan should not see too much of the "gang," continuing in true Emersonian fashion that "a man to make anything of himself has got to flock by himself." He went on, "You must survive for the glory of the old studio . . . You want to be a great artist, and you can if you only get yourself together—and for God's sake first give up running with the gang. The smart young men about us always seem to be so much wiser and look down on our youthful ambitions until if we go much amongst them we begin to doubt our fine old studio aspirations . . . I look back on them and on our old friendship in such a way that I cannot bear to think you could in any way give up. I have had few close friendships—yourself and Reddy the closest . . . Take care of yourself, then, John, for your own sake and for mine if for no other and don't in the heat of the thing ruin your chances of success and of life's happiness by any too hasty doings." Henri who, as Sloan said, "brought us into paint," watched over his friends with fatherly interest.

But Sloan had told Henri that he was lonely. "If I don't have some companionship," he said, "damned if I don't think I'll be driven into marriage"; and married, in the end, he was in 1901, not to the girl in question but to Dolly. Anna Wall, —her real name,—the daughter of an Irish immigrant who was supposed to have invented naphtha soap, of which he had been a prosperous manufacturer for a while, had been obliged to earn her living for a number of years already in the auditing department of Gimbel's. She was twenty-four when they were married, but Sloan had met her in 1898, introduced by the art director Edward Davis, and she had often come to the studio after parties to set things right and had even accompanied Sloan on a trip to New York. Tiny as a humming-bird, four feet nine inches tall, exactly the height of Queen Victoria, she was a tempestuous little soul, mercurial, unstable, but as bold as a jay in defence of her affections and beliefs. She was a manic-depressive and an alcoholic; and Sloan, who had no illusions about her, had much to put up with in the forty-two years of their life together. Often he was to write in his diary, with various cryptic comments, the word "wikefrund," an anagram for "wife drunk," when she came home without hat, purse or key, occasions when, as he once wrote, another person came to the front, an "evil, lying, mean" creature. But this was far less than half the story, for the "lonesome frightened little girl" whom John Sloan married when he was thirty had many admirable qualities for an artist's wife. Among them was the kind of devotion that led her always to insist on John Sloan's working solely to please himself. To help him at the outset she took him away from his family, obliging his sisters henceforth to look after themselves, and in time she played an important part in John Sloan's life-work, though she went rather beyond him in her pursuit of causes. Attempting suicide more than once, with strychnine or with veronal, consulting soothsayers and palmists all through life, with constant feelings of inferiority* in the presence of Sloan's educated friends, she

* Sloan said that one of his motives in keeping a diary was to contribute to Dolly's self-esteem. Knowing that she would read it, he constantly praised her as he wrote,—her housekeeping, her cooking,

was, as one of them said, Sloan's "outboard motor." For her quickness and activity were a valuable spur for a nature that was somewhat slow and somewhat passive.

So, at least, Sloan always felt, profoundly affectionate as he was, long-suffering, dependable and loyal, and, for the rest, on the whole, content with a relation that was not too romantic.* Working both afternoons and evenings, he saw few others, aside from his friends, and had small chance to observe the life of the streets; he had never even seen Walt Whitman, the old poet who died in 1893. Sloan had given Henri a fine copy of *Leaves of Grass* and Whitman from the first had been a bond between them; moreover, the poet had been visible often on Market Street during all the years when Sloan was growing up. Meanwhile, with little facility,—a limitation he did not regret,—but with what he called a kind of dogged patience, Sloan "hammered out" his paintings "with a great deal of effort," as he recorded in one of his later notes. He said his sister Marianna had more talent than himself and that he had more perseverance than skill, or, as he put it, "I had less ability than a lot of the others, so I had to work harder." Near-sighted, always wearing the glasses that he was to wear through life, for he had had trouble with his eyes from the age of twelve, he was already interested rather in getting "solidity" in his work than Henri's

---

her pursuit of causes,—making much of her to give her confidence in herself and keep her from melancholy and drinking.

* "I cannot honestly say that love comes first in my life. But I believe that a man who cares first of all for his work is apt to be a more loving husband than the one who is 'romantic.' His adventures are in the mind rather than social passions, and affection lasts with him."—One of Sloan's notes in later years.

"sensation of livingness in things." One might have thought that the influence of Eakins had reached him directly, as it undoubtedly reached him through the teaching of Anshutz; and he always remembered a remark of Eakins as the first intimation he had, when he was beginning to paint, that his work had some value. He had shown at the Pennsylvania Academy a picture called "The Look of a Woman," a dark murky thing, as he described it, for "we were painting that way then,—you had to 'get into' the picture to see it." But Eakins, noticing it, not knowing who the painter was, said, "That boy is going somewhere."

"I emerged into real interest in the life around me, with paint in my hand, *after* I came to New York," Sloan said once. "When I had city life work to do while drawing for the paper, it was just a 'job.' " But before he left Philadelphia he was well launched in his life-work, beginning with imitations of Frans Hals portraits, one of which he called "The Hungry Boy" and another "Boy with Piccolo." In much of the work of Frans Hals he was to feel in after years "just competent and rather honest paint slinging"; but at this time,—with Daumier and Leech,—Frans Hals, Velasquez and Manet were his gods because they were the gods of Henri also. Sloan never disputed the taste of this older painter to whom, as a disciple, he looked up, who had seen so much more of the world of art and who was a natural teacher and a natural leader. Beginning to paint "in darkest Henri,"—James Huneker's later phrase,—with motives that he called literary and poetic, he was already drawn to the street scenes that he so seldom observed and he painted a few of these following his portraits. Among them were "Independence Square," "The Old Walnut Street Theatre" and "East Entrance, City Hall," with the hay-cart, the hansom, the horses and the crossing-sweeper. He painted from memory, his invariable way, obeying the counsel of Henri, who invariably worked himself directly from nature, and always indifferent to "success," never expecting to live by the pictures that he painted for his own pleasure. Sloan, in fact, was not to sell a painting until he was forty-two, but he was already convinced that "art makes living worth while," as he said years later in *Gist of Art*. "It makes starving living. It makes worry, it makes trouble, it makes a life that would be barren of everything—living. Art brings life to life."

## CHAPTER IV

# NEW YORK: FIRST YEARS

JOHN SLOAN had gone over to New York, for a trial visit, in 1898, when Glackens, on the art staff of the New York *Herald*, arranged for him to have a position there; but, having said "yes," as he wrote to Henri, under the influence of two or three drinks, he had returned to the city of his boyhood and youth. "Don't think that I have been unable to hold my own in the metropolis," he added in this letter to his friend in Paris, "or that I have returned once more to sleep the sleep of Philadelphia. I have returned by my own wish . . . in order to be worked under *more pressure*." For in his experience an artist on the *Herald* did not know what work was beside an artist on his Philadelphia paper. While he had learned much in his three months in New York, he preferred to be "the big frog in the little puddle." Moreover, although Philadelphia was ugly compared to New York, he somehow felt "more like an artist" there.

So, although Henri had settled in New York in 1901 and most of the "old stock company" had long since gone there, Sloan did not make his final move until three years later, when he lived at first near Henri in the old Sherwood building.* It was "as though," he said, "the bronze creation

* The main reason why Sloan left the *Press* was that the Sunday magazine supplement for which he worked was replaced by a syndi-

of the elder Calder" had "left its perch on City Hall,"—the colossal statue of William Penn by Stirling Calder's father that was topped by a Quaker hat with a prodigious brim. Everett Shinn had executed a lively dance around this brim, or so he once averred in a convivial moment, but Sloan was more deliberate than the volatile Shinn who had gone to live in New York well before Henri. Even now Sloan was taking a chance with an order from the *Century Magazine* and little else to count on in the future; and, in fact, for several years the Sloans had only one regular source of income, the weekly puzzle he continued to draw for the *Press.** But, having made up his mind, he had no regrets, and, after revisiting Philadelphia, for a glimpse of his invalid mother, he was always glad to come back to the "great life-full city." Now and then, as he wrote in his diary,† Philadelphia pleased him with its "livable, lovable old look, though impossible of course," but, liking the centre of the town, he said it was a very small centre and he hated the

---

cated one. The others had previously lost their jobs when the half-tone process enabled camera-men to do their work.

During the years 1899-1902, almost every Sunday issue of the *Press* contained a full page in colour executed by Sloan.

While Philadelphia had once been a great centre of magazines, most of them by 1904 were published in New York. It was practically important for illustrators to be within reach of the editors if they wished to make a living as free lances.

* "I used to make puzzles, you know. Take ten words, names of pieces of furniture and then captions and drawings to work them out from. Two Englishmen talking, so far . . . sofa."—John Sloan, note for *Gist of Art*.

† Sloan began keeping a diary in 1906 and continued it through 1914. He did not resume it again until the last five years of his life, 1946-1951.

city's "miles of dingy small 'homes.'" Philadelphia figured in his mind at moments as "that beastly hole," while New York had "a happy look" and the people had "a happy air," perhaps because many had come from other countries.*

In any case, arriving in New York, he saw the life of the people more than he had previously seen it, as he noted later, because in Philadelphia he had lived at home and worked on the paper steadily from two in the afternoon till eleven at night. He had even liked to work on Sunday instead of taking the day off, and, as a result of this routine, he had never loafed and invited his soul, never turned himself "loose among the people," in Whitman's fashion; while he found it exciting and wonderful now to have whole days to himself to wander about the streets and see new things. Roaming the metropolis for a decade to come, he saw its life as Balzac had seen Paris. Sloan loved Balzac,—"If you were marooned on a desert island, reading Balzac would make you a citizen of the world," he said; and, like Dreiser, who also loved Balzac, he saw the life about him in all its native character, texture and grain. Others,—Childe Hassam, for instance,—who were also enthralled by the New York scene, always contrived to make it look like Paris; but, with all his own reading of Balzac, and Paul de Kock as well, Sloan's

* Sloan often spoke of "the usual contrast between Philadelphia and New York with the usual victory for the latter." On one of his visits to Philadelphia he noted in his diary a picture he had observed from the car window,—"A young well-dressed woman whose old grey-haired mother was seeing her off on the New York train. Silent yearning under control on the mother's part and eagerness to get back to the city in every action of the younger woman who did not want to hurt the mother but who wouldn't have stayed for anything—quite right."

clear eye saw New York in its own essence. He saw it as Alfred Stieglitz saw it in his photographs of New York streets, "The Terminal," "Winter—Fifth Avenue," "Five Points," wintry scenes, scenes in the slums and of immigrants on sidewalks, witnessed with a similar indigenous integrity and truth. A few years were to make Sloan not only the "Manhattan Constantin Guys" but what somebody else called him, the "American Hogarth," an epithet that pleased him although, as it happened, Sloan himself had never seen an original Hogarth in colour.*

Soon settled in his "garret," the top floor of the shabby old house, 165 West Twenty-third Street, Sloan had begun the life of constant observation and varied work that was to make him quintessentially the New York painter. Henri, meanwhile, returning from Paris and leaving Philadelphia had taught for a while with William M. Chase; then he had set up a school of his own in the Lincoln Arcade,—a Latin Quarter in itself,—on upper Broadway. There, in this rookery of half-fed students, astrologers, prostitutes, actors, models, prize-fighters, quacks and dancers, Henri had begun his great years of teaching, the arch-radical and high priest of

* When, many years later, Sloan saw Hogarths for the first time, —at an exhibition of Hogarth, Constable and Turner in the Metropolitan Museum, 1947,—he wrote, "I realize now what a compliment was paid me by those critics who called me the American Hogarth." Adding that the Hogarth owned by the museum was "obviously a 'hack' job," he said these pictures were "full of wonderful human detail with a beautiful managing of neutral colours." He noted the "fine differences in complexion" and the frequent use of "repainted greys." He continued, "In Hogarth there are times when his insistence on detail retards the flow of the design. Sometimes he has a very fine sense of chiaroscuro." He added, "I'm glad to see that the 'Shrimp Girl' is as poor a picture as I've always thought."

all the rebels against the "genteel tradition." These were the young painters who were bent on "slapping down pretty art," the phrase of George Luks with which they would all have agreed,—George Bellows, Edward Hopper, Rockwell Kent, Guy Pène du Bois, Glenn O. Coleman, Gifford Beal and Walter Pach. Others were Walt Kuhn, William Gropper and Vachel Lindsay, the Illinois poet,—like Henri himself, a devotee of Whitman,—whose gift for rhythms and words Henri recognized at once. He counselled Lindsay to give up painting for it. Most of these younger men were sooner or later friends of Sloan, who said Henri was "as proud as a hen with a brood of ducks," telling them that painting was a man's vocation, not for the tender-minded or the half-hearted. He made them see things and want to make pictures of scenes, people, incidents that were exciting, interesting, amusing or sad. Henri, moreover, taught them to see whatever was great in their native tradition, at least in the work of the preëminent writers and artists.

For years, whenever Sloan was asked where a young man should study art, he always said, "With Henri, none other"; and he was surprised in 1908 when Stuart Davis stopped in one day to ask him where he could find the Art Students' League. How could he think of going to the League when he knew that Henri had a school? The answer was that Edward Davis, Sloan's old Philadelphia friend, regarded the Henri school as "far too advanced"; but, however Sloan felt later about it, or about Henri's teaching, he taught there himself when Henri was away. At these times he zealously gave his whole day to the teaching, hoping that his revered Henri's work might be carried forward in the master's absence and anxious, as he said, to give the students something for their development "in the way of ideas." Henri restlessly wandered about, travelling and painting in Holland and Spain, looking for people who were exciting to paint, the bull-fighter Asiego, the Spanish dancer La Reina Mora, the Spanish officer in the blue uniform and helmet. He painted these subjects, Sloan said, without any "taint of the picturesque,"—they all had the "good sound life of the animal in them,"—while Henri wrote that the sky in Holland was varied and active with a blue-grey warmth that was unlike any other he had seen. The evening sky especially was of a transparent deep blue that added greatly to the beauty of the night street scenes. The young painter Randall Davey was there with him and Eugene Speicher had passed through with his bride. Then Henri was in England, in Halifax, painting a portrait of the wife of the mayor and sketching the house in which Sterne wrote *A Sentimental Journey* near Robin Hood's legendary grave on the Yorkshire moorland. Returning, Henri brought Sloan wonderful sets of Goya's etchings, the *Caprichos, Desastres* and *Proverbios,* all three collections, with Rembrandt etchings and a book on Félicien Rops.

The "crowd," meantime, who had come to New York because life looked larger there, were working more or less along Sloan's lines,—Glackens, for one, who was drawing scenes of tenements, fire-escapes, push-carts, while Luks did comic drawings for the *Journal* and the *World.* Painting again, he would say, "The world never had but two artists, Frans Hals and little old George Luks," with frequent remarks like "Art—my slats! Guts! Guts! Life! Life! I can paint with a shoe-string dipped in pitch and lard." Working with both hands equally well, he was to produce soon "The New York Cabby," "The Bread-Winners," "Knitters in the Park," with scenes of the Gansevoort docks in winter or pictures from the mines like "The Breaker Boy," recalling the low-life pictures of the old Dutch painters. With "The Wrestlers" he was going to show what anatomy really was to those "pink and white idiots," Will Low and Kenyon Cox. Glackens, who had been painting dark pictures under Henri's influence, had broken into full colour in 1904 when he came back from Paris full of Rubens and Renoir. At present, like Sloan, he was drawing in reaction against Maxfield Parrish and Howard Pyle and their costumed heroes of historical and swashbuckling romances. The versatile Shinn, who was painting already his lovely night pastels, sometimes with an ash-can in sight,—his finest pictures,—was busy with mechanics and money-making too, decorating theatres, pianos and screens, while experimenting with small models of an aeroplane. To Sloan his cleverness seemed "demonic," with his miniature stage-settings in which rocks, cliffs, lighthouses, drawbridges and moats were placed in a proscenium with various lighting effects; and at the same time, with terrific speed, he executed in two weeks a big Watteau-like tapestry painting. He decorated the house of Stanford White, who arranged for his first one-man show, but he was always thinking of gadgets, a windshield-wiper for eye-glasses, a contraption to remove lead from paper and restore it to the pencil; another was a trellis that rolled up at night, folding the flowering vines in a box in which an insecticide sprayed the blossoms until morning. Meanwhile, appearing on the stage himself, he was writing the comic melodramas one of which was played for eighteen years. A great lover of hansom cabs, Shinn was always rushing away to see some "ten-millionaire" up-town, but whenever they met Sloan warmed to him, different as Shinn had become from the scalawag with whom he had worked in former years. There could have been no greater contrast than that between the sparkling Shinn and the reserved and quietly witty Glackens.

It was Glackens who had suggested Sloan as the co-illustrator of a translated edition of Paul de Kock, the novelist whose scenes of Parisian life in the days of Balzac and the Restoration must have sharpened Sloan's own eye for the world about him. Sloan had made more than fifty etchings and as many drawings for this series of books,—to which Glackens, Luks and Shinn contributed also,—pictures of French popular urban life that were quite in tune with his representation of the streets, dance-halls and parks of his own adopted city.* Magazine editors at that time were looking for really good illustrations to match in directness and honesty the writings of the moment,—the work of the realistic story-tellers and the "muckrakers"; and, devoted as Sloan was to drawing and etching, they chose him for sad, grim and humorous city-life pictures. Among others, he illustrated stories of Brand Whitlock and Ernest Poole and occasionally an "Irish humour" story. His first illustration for the *Century,* which had led him to settle in New York, had been a drawing of a man sawing lumber on a roof, a

* These illustrations of Paul de Kock were Sloan's first important etchings. He had produced them before he left Philadelphia. Later, in 1911, Sloan illustrated six of Gaboriau's novels in English translations.

subject as remote as one could imagine from the work of the popular Howard Pyle and what Sloan called his "poor little imitation hæmorrhoids of pupils." But this was the kind of subject to which he gave significance in many of his illustrations in *Scribner's* and *Harper's,* in *Everybody's, Collier's, Munsey's* and the *Saturday Evening Post,** and in the *Canzoni* of T. A. Daly, whom he had known in Philadelphia and whose " 'cute,' clever" poems he interpreted in black and white.

There was one kind of picturesque drawing or etching Sloan was careful to avoid, for he said it was abhorrent to a man of real social feeling,—those "sentimental scrawlings of bearded Jews" in which "seven thousand years of suffering" were "expressed in a rotten line with sloppy tones." Or drawings of Negroes by Southerners who "just loved" the downtrodden. In all this kind of work, said Sloan, the artist was showing superiority, a cheap kind of condescension that was never present in the work of Millet or Daumier. Sloan's "system," as he described it, of making a living was to call on the editors for orders and establish for himself a deadline for the drawings; then, painting steadily until the last minute, he would do the drawings, collect the money and pay his rent and other bills. The feeling of being in debt made it impossible for him to work at anything but jobs that would bring in the necessary money, while it was against his grain to borrow from friends; and he called this "letting the work of illustrating push me in my painting." The system which he adopted worked very well, for his period of greatest ac-

* "The magazine that looks and feels like a dead fish."—One of Sloan's "student notes."

tivity as an illustrator was the period in which he produced the majority of "Sloans." This became the popular name for his city-life paintings.

These were great days for black-and-white artists when Boardman Robinson, who became Sloan's friend, was creating a kind of cartoon that was robust and free, very unlike the meticulous work not only of Sloan's "poisonous" Howard Pyle but of most of the older school of illustrators. Influenced by Forain in some degree and by Rembrandt's drawings, especially, which he had studied intently, at first in the Louvre, Robinson felt that a drawing should be a composition in just the same fashion that a painting should be. His illustrations in the *Morning Telegraph*, which one admirer characterized as "like young oaks in a forest of weary willows," were, Sloan said, "a great inspiration to me"; and another cartoonist who became Sloan's friend, much as they differed in various ways, was the liberal politically minded Rollin Kirby. With Kirby he often walked in the afternoons, stopping in one day at Durand Ruel's to see a fine showing of Monets there. This friend had a great collection of Charles Keene's work, some of it rare, though Sloan put Leech above Keene as a "freer thinker," considering him, as he wrote in his diary, "Rembrandt's peer in line work" and the finest possible example of the "clean artist mind." He spent evenings studying Keene and others, as he noted, "gloating over my Daumier lithographs" in the twelve volumes of *Charivari* that he bought in 1906 containing nearly eight hundred of Daumier's best. These particular volumes, which were also full of Gavarni, had once belonged to the brothers Goncourt. Later Sloan loaned them to the print department of the

Metropolitan Museum and finally, during the great depression, he sold them.

In most of Sloan's work in black and white one felt a kindly humour,—one of his mottoes was "Draw with human kindness,"—in spite of the quick and bitter tongue that he admitted he possessed and as one might have supposed from some of his etchings. One of these was the well-known plate, the "Fifth Avenue Critics" of 1905, the most popular perhaps of all his etchings; and in many of his other records of snobbery or sham one found a similar justly satiric note. Careful always to avoid mixing polemics with painting, he observed that he always made an etching when he had something "vitriolic" to say, and he disdained the word "charm" * and suspected the word "beauty" as having something meretricious and equivocal about it. He was rather pleased than otherwise when the old art critic Russell Sturgis said that his Paul de Kock etchings were lacking in charm, and when Sturgis, examining his New York plates, said "Turning out the Light" had charm, Sloan felt there must be something the matter with it. He preferred Howard Pyle's remark,—evasive as Pyle otherwise was as the art editor of *McClure's*, when Sloan had called on him,—that his work was "good in character"; while, "sourish or kindly," mostly the latter, Sloan's etchings, if not a means of support, were his main interest, second only to painting.

The first of Sloan's New York city plates was "Connoisseurs of Prints" and another was the plate of the copyist in the museum, painting a picture of sheep with a crowd about

* "Whistler turned etchings into boutonnières," Sloan said in *Gist of Art*.

her, while these were the years of "Love on the Roof," "Swinging in the Square," "The Little Bride," "The Show Case," "Jewelry Store Window" and dozens of others. In one of these an old woman finds corsets in an ash-barrel, in another one sees the "Nickelodeon" with a group of girls having "fun, one cent"; another, "The Man-Monkey," recalled the one-man band with the organ-grinder whom Sloan had seen so often in the Chelsea side-streets. Sloan made his etchings from drawings carefully worked out on tissue-paper, which he then treated with paraffin to make it transparent, afterwards tracing the outline on the plate, though his later plates were needled directly on the copper. He had become known as an etcher very early. Of his Paul de Kock etchings, Arthur B. Davies had said, "Nothing better has ever been done," and Henri had written to him in 1903 from South Carolina: "I wish you could know on what a plane these etchings of yours have placed you in the minds of many, very many who know. The word 'master' is what generally comes to express the opinion of them, and you know what a daring thing it is to say of anyone who hasn't been heralded as such from afar." Seven years later six of Sloan's etchings were exhibited in Paris in the spring Salon.*

* "Albert Sterner came in . . . Wanted to see my etchings. He spoke very appreciatively of them. Said it did him good to come into a studio where the work was free from commercialism."—John Sloan's diary, 1906.

It was another older artist, Henry W. Ranger, the landscape painter, who bought the first set of his city etchings that Sloan ever sold.

Mahonri Young later said that there was a marked difference between Sloan's etchings and those of most of his contemporaries. "His plates are never sketches, they are complete works, as serious works

During these years Robert Henri and his wife Linda were often with the Sloans either in West Twenty-third Street or the Sherwood building, in the Henri studio that became the setting of the etching called "Memory" that Sloan made in 1906 after Linda's death. In this the four are gathered together around the old table from the Charcoal Club with the bowl of fruit, the matches and the cards in the centre and the box of cigars on the shelf behind Henri, who is sketching in the big armchair while Sloan sketches opposite, pipe in mouth. Dolly, chin in hands, looks out from the centre and Linda, with her arm on the table, is reading aloud, a scene that was still characteristic of many an evening at the Sloans' after Linda died and Henri had been left to live alone.* Henri would often draw while Sloan worked on a puzzle and Dolly, sitting beside them, read aloud from *Tess of the D'Urbervilles* or Maupassant's *Fort comme la Mort*, though sometimes Dolly played solitaire or worked on coloured silk shirts for Sloan with button-holes that he said were "rather pathetic." For the button-holes looked like "wobbly eyelashes."

From time to time, quite often, Dolly returned to Philadelphia in search of cures for her nerves, consulting doctors, for, having no children and no causes to serve, she was living at this period in a state of constant neurotic tension. But Sloan, who felt "aimless" when she was away, as he felt she kept him going, was happy when she bustled about with

---

as important pictures or statues, or, shall we say, as novels or symphonies."

* Two years later Henri married Marjorie Organ, a cartoonist on the New York *Journal* and *World* who especially satirized the foibles of New York women.

the carpet-sweeper and came every now and then to give him a kiss, and he worked all day once making a copper plate into a buckle design for a hat for Dolly. Another day he made the "tank," his box for portfolios and drawing paper, or he spent an evening cutting out mats for etchings, and often he and Henri worked together at the etching-press, having, as he wrote, "a little monotype fun." Once Dolly dictated the expurgated parts of George Moore's *Memoirs of My Dead Life,* reading them from the English edition that Moore had given to Huneker, while Henri wrote them into an American copy. Meanwhile, the two friends walked together of an afternoon, perhaps to the Anderson Auction Rooms where Sloan picked up some fine old French paper and a lot of Japan paper at the same time. Sloan liked to play cards, poker, hearts, casino, and he often played golf with Rollin Kirby or Henri on the municipal links at Van Cortlandt Park. Henri wrote from South Carolina, where he was painting two portraits, that he was playing not golf but tennis there, and that, unlike golf, tennis was not a "philosopher's game." He added, "Golf might have its Izaak Walton. Tennis could only have a Beau Brummell." Sloan replied, "You make my hands itch for the grip of a driver, the swing from the spine, the crisp click of the contact, and then the long easy slice to the impenetrable, inscrutable rough at the right of the fair green."

But games were a passing phase with Sloan, who had never been a sportsman and who as a boy had always preferred reading to baseball; and even now, busy as he was, he spent many hours reading, ranging over a largish variety of books. He said he had never been so moved by a novel as he was by *Tess,* but he delighted in George Moore also, in *Confessions of a Young Man,* for one, and *The Lake,*—"splendid . . . it suits me perfectly," he said. Then there was Zola's *Thérèse Raquin, Madame Bovary, Tom Jones,* Arthur Morrison's *Child of the Jago,* H. G. Wells's *Tono-Bungay,* Ibsen's *The Wild Duck* and *Brand* and Meredith's *Diana of the Crossways.* In Philadelphia he had bought six volumes of the *Yellow Book,* with Kipling, Browning, Stockton, Molière and Poe; and he picked up Taine's *English Literature* and read it with zest, and at least five or six plays of Bernard Shaw. There were certain other books he had to read in order to obtain information for his illustrations, and he had made an elaborate study of the life, customs and costumes of Restoration Paris to prepare for his illustrations of Paul de Kock. He went into this so thoroughly that he said he knew from maps almost every street in Paris. He knew Paris almost as well as the streets of New York.

CHAPTER V

# THE WINDOW WATCHER

ONE OF THE BOOKS that Sloan enjoyed was Fielding's *Joseph Andrews*. When, for the second time, he was finishing this, it set him "thinking how necessary it is for an artist of any creative sort to go among *common people*—not to waste his time among his fellows, for it must be from the other class—not creators, nor Bohemians, nor dilettanti—that he will get his knowledge of life."

Here Sloan described his own everyday practice as a tireless roamer about New York who was painting and etching the life that he saw in the streets, and it seemed odd in later days that, with all his reading, he read so few of the writers whose work seemed closely allied to his. For the painters of the "Eight," or the "Ash-can School," as Sloan and his friends were to be called, had obviously much in common with a large group of writers, newspaper men turned story-tellers who lived, or had lived, in New York with similar youthful experiences and mature interests. Quite as varied as Sloan's associates, differing as Glackens differed from Luks, or as Everett Shinn differed from any of the others, Stephen Crane and Theodore Dreiser were both metropolitan realists, and so were the muckrakers and O. Henry. The "lure of the great cities," in a phrase of the moment, attracted both writers and painters who were sometimes equally described as "apostles of the ugly," together with a wish to see "how the other half lives," another phrase that influenced imaginative minds. For the rest, "Write of those things of which you know most and for which you care most," Hamlin Garland had said, following Howells, words that expressed the spirit of the age for writers and painters* alike, many of whom also felt the *nostalgie de la boue*. Eager to escape from a bourgeois world, they felt the attraction of mud and dirt, the slums, the bread-line and the morgue, and they were prepared to find the Bowery "the most interesting street in New York" where Stephen Crane said he had got his "artistic education." Theodore Roosevelt upbraided the writers who were less interested in Fulton Market than they were in the Renaissance market-place of Florence, and Walt Whitman alone, he said, had found in the Bowery what Dante would have found there if he had lived in our time. "What infinite use," Roosevelt exclaimed, "Dante would have made of the Bowery,"† and the new painters and writers shared Roosevelt's feeling.

But, equally stirred by the *zeitgeist,* possessed by similar themes and scenes, the painters and the writers were scarcely aware of one another, and, while Sloan had illustrated Stephen Crane's *Great Battles of the World* in 1901, he

* Sloan, who did not recall being influenced by Howells or Garland, said this influence "could have come to him through Henri."

† "The Bowery is one of the great highways of humanity, a highway of seething life, of varied interest, of fun, of work, of sordid and terrible tragedy; and it is haunted by demons as evil as any that stalk through the pages of the *Inferno.*"—Theodore Roosevelt, *Dante in the Bowery,* in *Historical Essays.*

knew nothing of this writer's stories until many years later.* Similarly, he left no record of having read O. Henry, for whom so many of his drawings might have served as illustrations, just as, for instance, his own picture "The Coffee Line" was a natural illustration for Stephen Crane. Again, encountering Theodore Dreiser, he was to express a marked distaste both for the man and for much of his work, although in some ways Dreiser and Sloan were akin; while he seldom read for pleasure the muckraker novelists whose stories he illustrated in the magazines. He said he had been

* Sloan seems to have read Stephen Crane's stories for the first time in 1948, when they were brought to him by a professor who was attempting to trace in a book the relations of these "realistic" painters and writers. In his diary of that year he wrote as follows, "I am finishing Stephen Crane's famous *Red Badge of Courage* which Dr. K. gave me along with a book of Crane's short stories written later. He wants me to catch up on these realistic writings and tell him if I as a 'realist' in painting of the early 20 years of this century feel any kindred motives. I cannot say I do as far as I know."

Sloan liked *Maggie* and *The Open Boat,* but he remarked that he did not care greatly for *The Red Badge of Courage.* With his general dislike of war as a subject, he found it rather immature and, as his wife reported, "old-fashioned in style." He also said that Crane's work gave him the same feeling as John Dos Passos's *Manhattan Transfer,* —"nostalgia for the New York of the days before automobiles and prohibition." He said further that "Crane's attitude was human rather than socially conscious," adding, "I think he really loved the down and outs on the Bowery, out of his love for all life." This might have been said of Sloan himself.

In 1950, Sloan wrote again: "It is now the fad to trace a connection between our work and that of Dreiser, Norris and Crane. As far as I know, there was no direct contact, certainly not in the nineties. We came to realism in revolt against sentimentality and artificial subject-matter and the cult of 'art for art's sake' . . . We read realist writers like Zola and Ibsen more than Americans who were beginning to work this field."

"too preoccupied" to read many American writers, although he had had time for Rider Haggard, not to mention Stevenson and Kipling, a point that was only interesting later because it symbolized a time when the new American mind was still divided. What came to be called "the American scene,"—a phrase that Sloan disliked,—engrossed the imagination of both writers and painters, but their cultural interests remained almost wholly European.

Meanwhile, insatiably curious and deeply sympathetic, Sloan rambled every day through the New York streets, where he might have met Dreiser or Sydney Porter whom the city stirred to write as it stirred him to paint, with so many of his friends. It aroused what he called "the joy of the painter-poet," for he was just like "an innocent poet," he said. He painted things he "saw with interest," not with any conscious feeling that he must paint city life but because it perpetually quickened, amused and touched him. Each of his pictures originated in some emotional experience, he wrote, adding that he always had to see some human incident before he wanted to paint a picture. For, busy as he was with etching and drawing in black and white, his passion, his ambition was to paint, and, pleased as he was to illustrate a good book like *The Moonstone,** he was happiest of all with his palette and brushes. It irked him to have lucrative orders that kept him from them, and, comparing himself and his closest friends with most of the artists

* "When planning illustrations for a book," Sloan wrote in one of his notes, "first I read it through for mood, then again for action and description, marking the passages which strike me most. After this I go through and plan the drawings to fall at intervals through the text."

in *Life, Judge* and *Puck,* he asked why and how they differed so greatly. They were all alike "handling American life," but these others "didn't have something that brought out the painter in the rest of us," the something that to Sloan seemed to be "contact with Henri."

As for his own special beat, if he may be said to have had one, it was not so much the Bowery,—which interested him also,—as West Fourteenth Street and lower Sixth Avenue, "drab, shabby, happy, sad and human." There stood the Haymarket, one of his themes, and, walking up to Henri's, he passed what he called a humorous sight of interest, the hairdresser's window, which he presently painted, with the crowd watching below while the stout blonde manipulator bleached the hair of a client. Sixth Avenue had for Sloan a "Coney Island quality,"—he called it "the Fifth Avenue of the poor" that "furnished similar facilities at lower rates"; and there he observed on another occasion a crowd looking at a "sheath gown" in a window. This much talked of innovation from Paris was open to the knee and the wax figure had a queer wooden leg showing. Sixth Avenue and Fourteenth Street were the haunt of the street-walkers who sauntered back and forth swinging their bags, often with long feathers, and Sloan remembered one who wore a pair of plumes that were like great horns. These made her look like "some wild creature of the night." Sloan walked by the hour up and down Sixth Avenue, sometimes following the crowd into a burlesque theatre where he noted once a very amusing "yaller gal," a buck-and-wing dancer whom he hoped to paint. He studied the cigar-store wooden Indians that struck, for him, a higher average of art than most of the contemporary American sculpture,—which seemed to him like chewing-gum on a large scale,*—and he often went out of his way to see these wooden figures. His favourite was a wooden maiden in front of an Eighth Avenue shop at about Twenty-fifth Street.

While, for the rest, he was not averse to dining at Mouquin's with the crowd,—or with Henri near Times Square at Shanley's or Churchill's,—he usually resorted to restaurants on a humbler level, and when he and Dolly went out in the evening it was often to the "Cave Parisienne" or the "25 cent table d'hôte across the street." He sometimes referred in his diary to the "decent Hungarian dinner" for which they also paid twenty-five cents or to the little Eighth Avenue bakery that had "very nice food—twenty cents each." He had no objection to lobster Newburgh and the best white wine or luxurious dinners at the houses of prosperous friends,—for instance, Glackens's on Washington Square where everything, he wrote, was "so rich and fine," thanks to Mrs. Glackens's family silk business. But he felt that Glackens's high living would not have been good for him, any more than Everett Shinn's "plush grottoes," and, finding subjects in restaurants of many kinds, he found them oftenest in unpretentious places. He painted Gonfarone's and Renganeschi's,—the "restaurant of the republic of San Marino," a stone's throw from the Jefferson Market

* This was one of Sloan's favourite pleasantries. In a speech later in life he referred ironically to chewing-gum as a form of sculpture, saying, "It's casual, its unpremeditated. Collect chewing-gum before it's been stepped on, put each bit in a glass case, with chromium on it, and you'd find individuality, as good as autographs if the chewers were known."

gaol,—and the Chinese restaurant, gorgeous with teak-wood, mother of pearl and gold, where he saw the girl feeding her boy friend before taking him home. There he saw another with "dashing red feathers" playing with a cat who became the theme of a painting four weeks later. But he and Dolly especially liked the restaurant of Romany Marie, or the series of restaurants in Christopher Street and elsewhere, kept by this feminine counsellor, philosopher and friend of so many Greenwich Villagers of that lively epoch. A great friend of Dolly's, Romany Marie kept young, Sloan said, with her interest in others, and she said later that Sloan was different from all the other artists of his time in having "such warmth and feeling for people." * Sloan made an etching of Romany Marie's, a little restaurant of a type that vanished, he was to note, as the century advanced, and he made five paintings of McSorley's "Old Ale House" on East Seventh Street, near Cooper Union.† He sometimes stopped for a

* Sloan painted a portrait of Romany Marie, "the only portrait of me that wasn't sensational," she said. Later she added, in a newspaper interview, Sloan "looked at me and said, 'I'm going to paint you as an earthy little girl coming to our shores to put herself over.' That's John Sloan. He always had a sense of humanity. I was just a kid then, here from Roumania, trying to get along."

† About McSorley's,—the "old standby,"—Sloan said he felt as Edgar Lee Masters felt about *Spoon River*,—he could not "get away from it."

In connection with "McSorley's, Saturday Night," he noted in a catalogue that during prohibition the bar was never closed. The only difference was that the mugs became smaller, the prices higher and the crowd was larger. It was always conducted, he said, with "dignity and decorum."

In 1940 he noted further that the present proprietor had a colour reproduction of the "now famous painting." He wanted an autographed photograph of Sloan to hang beside it on the wall, saying customers were always asking why it was not there.

glass of ale at this venerable tavern with sawdust on the floor and sporting and theatrical prints around the walls, where the sun streamed in the front door and windows, lighting up the sawdust and the soft and gentle faces of the Irish patrons. Painting the bar, he also painted the back room where old John McSorley, with his five-toed cat, philosophized and entertained his friends, among them Art Young and the "villager" Hippolyte Havel who, along with the artist, appeared in Sloan's picture. Sloan said that McSorley's was a "temple of temperance" where one could drink only ale, where there were no mixed drinks and no women were admitted and there was neither time nor turmoil.

Now Sloan was an "incorrigible window watcher," as he wrote once in a catalogue, and the back windows of the attic studio in West Twenty-third Street afforded many a scene that appeared in his work. There was an array of roofs where tenement women hung out their wash and sometimes made love or slept on summer nights, there were back yards where stray cats took part in human dramas and there were animated windows, a dozen or a score. Some were the windows of rooming-houses with tenants that constantly changed but not before they had told Sloan a story, and there, especially when the night was warm, human nature disported itself in a fashion that delighted the eye of an etcher and painter. There was one curious two-room household with two men and two women who cooked at three in the morning and whose day began at midnight, and there was a careless couple, the woman with carrot-red hair, who lay on the bed naked playing with a kitten. The woman wiggled her toes and the kitten jumped at them, while at intervals the couple drank from a stone jug of beer. There was another couple, a fat blonde woman and a thin man who had lost one hand and whom Sloan took for a gangster, and there were two girls in nightgowns that clung close to their backs who washed their breakfast dishes at twelve o'clock noon. For Sloan their nightgowns were full of the humour of life. He painted from memory afterwards a girl who leaned out on a window-sill, and he noted another girl combing her hair whom he saw in conjunction with a cat on the leads outside. He observed a boy at a mirror making faces at himself and a young girl bathing, half hidden by a door; and one night he watched another small drama, a half-dressed girl at a window and a man on the roof surveying her charms. This man was smoking a pipe while at another window below his wife was hanging out his newly washed linen. Sloan once saw a baby die in its mother's arms while the men of the family stood by, stupid and helpless. She held the baby in her arms after it had started to pale and stiffen, hope trying to fight off fact until fact killed hope and the men, sympathetic with her anguish, took it from her. Sloan could "hear nothing," he wrote, "but the acting was perfect."

Sometimes these stories that made pictures for Sloan went on from night to night, for three weeks in one case that he recorded in which a young man played cat and mouse with a dishevelled young woman and finally agreed to patch up his quarrel with her. When he left she nursed her rage and grief with tumblers of dark beer, but the young man kept reappearing,—with his narrow face, slim nose and raw umber hair,—packing suitcases and going again, after stripping the sheets from the bed, then suddenly coming back when the girl was asleep.* But while the windows across the way, and the populated roofs, afforded many subjects, with girls drying their hair, old women hanging out clothes, boys playing games,—pigeons at rest or flying, stealthy cats,—Sloan found these on every side, at five-cent moving picture shows, at the Hippodrome, at variety shows with Harry Lauder. ("A manly sturdy little fellow," wrote Sloan, "his costumes so well conceived, over whom the house went wild when he sang 'I love a lassie.' ") He found them at Procter's, with Trixie Friganza, at "leg shows," with "girls in tights . . . a bad kind of imitation nude," and in the Bowery, at the People's Theatre, where he heard an Italian performance of *Rigoletto*. "The Bowery, that name! so romantic," wrote Sloan, "to the youth of towns in the U.S.," which seemed only a name one wintry night, "so dull and dark and safe and slushy," while on other occasions it produced for him "a maze of living incidents . . . more than my brain could comprehend." One rainy evening he watched there a poor decrepit drunken wretch, with hat off and his mouth dripping saliva, in a cracked cackle cheering the Stars and Stripes hung out over a cheap eating-house. Another day he observed the crowd about a large wagon with paper boxes and small tongues of flame coming

* "Psychologists say that artists have a streak of the 'Peeping Tom' in their make-up. Perhaps it is true, but in a healthy sense."—One of Sloan's unpublished notes.

"I am in the habit of *watching every bit* of human life I can see about my windows, but I do it so that I am not observed at it . . . No insult to the people you are watching to do so unseen."—Sloan's diary, 1911.

through the heart-shaped opening behind the driver's seat; and he watched a Negro girl watching cats and a boy who exclaimed over a wagon-load of crates, "My, I wish I had that wood!" The lower East Side delighted him, even the doorways, greasy and begrimed, that looked as if hogs, covered with filth, had worn the paint away, going in and out. He once saw a boy spitting at a shabby old hearse. But he loved to watch happy healthy girls swinging in the parks there and boys playing jackstones and marbles on sidewalks and steps, —or pouring out of schools carrying violin-cases,—children with solid legs and rich full colour in their hair, suggesting rather happiness than misery in the East Side life. Fifth Avenue faces struck him as unhappy beside them. He liked the vendor-stands at night with flaring torches, smoky and red, the big price-placards of the butcher shops and the brilliant array of vegetables under the red-yellow glare of the electric lights.

Sloan strolled through the New York streets several miles every day, alert for sights and incidents that would make good pictures, for it was always some human incident that made him see the picture and he never painted places without people in them. He was convinced that a literary motive might inspire the finest art, that in fact it almost always did so; and he believed that "an interest in things is and always was at the root of art." He painted scenes he had glimpsed through windows while riding on elevated trains, remembering the kind of place it was, getting the character of the whole room as well as the human beings in it. He noted the sturdiness of a chair, the delicacy of muslin curtains blowing in a window, the heat, the tired look of the rug on the floor.* He studied the "Lafayette" at night, with its nineteenth century atmosphere, the old "wigwam" of Tammany Hall in its dingy red brick and the searchlight from Madison Square Garden "scratching the belly of the sky," as he wrote, and glaring in the faces of the promenaders. Once on Twenty-sixth Street he saw eyes behind the slats of shutters and a soft voice called him,—"a good subject for a plate"; and a girl, perhaps bibulous, certainly blithe, lifted her skirts as he passed and leaped a street hydrant on gloomy Twenty-fourth Street. He watched, on Second Avenue, the diners on the balcony of the Café Boulevard, and, walking on the mall in Central Park, he was amused by a crowd of boys who were running races about the fountain. The leader and director was a fair-haired boy who ran in one of the races himself and vindicated his own claims by running like the wind as compared with any of the others. He noticed a modish woman laughing at the dresses of some Indian squaws who crossed Fifth Avenue at Thirty-fourth Street and who seemed to Sloan more rationally rigged than she was, interesting as he found other women's dresses and the dashing large hats that went with the style of the moment. He noted that he must keep an eye out for a rich woman entering a Fifth Avenue bank, feeling there must be "something" in that for him. Then he liked the noon hour on lower Fifth Avenue on a brilliant sunny day when the street was full of bare-headed girl cloth-

* "Think of drawing as a way of talking about the things that interest you. Think of those wonderful documents, drawings made on scraps of paper by the lesser Dutch masters while they were wandering around market places and sitting in saloons."—John Sloan, *Gist of Art.*

ing workers, and especially the drama of the Flatiron building when there was a high wind and the gusts played pranks with the women's summer dresses. Sometimes their skirts flapped over their heads and two mounted policemen and two on foot were stationed at points of vantage there to keep men from loitering and watching too much and too long.

That favourite corner of the wind and the dust was one of John Sloan's chosen spots, overlooking his beloved Madison Square, with the old Fifth Avenue Hotel facing the fresh greenery and the hansoms and horse-drawn busses plodding by. He was fond also of Washington Square where the young girls at the lunch hour strolled about the paths arm in arm and benches were filled with all sorts and conditions of men, interested in the girls and not interested in them; but at this period of his life Madison Square was nearer home and he often sat and loafed there at all seasons of the year. In springtime when the buds were breaking out and the leaves unfolding on the trees he observed the men setting out pansies in the large circular bed, while the people stopped and watched them as they had stopped in the city of his youth when he painted the first picture he exhibited, "Independence Square." In summer, on his usual morning walk around to Broadway for the Sunday papers, he would sit for an hour or two on a bench in the square when the trees were heavily daubed with green and only a few seats were filled with bums and the streets had the bald hot vacant Sunday look. In the grey sunlight the dresses of the women, as they passed, whether pink, blue, green or yellow, looked somehow chalky; then later he would come again to watch the summer waning when dresses, like the trees, seemed full of colour. This, with the colour of the brass trimmings of the automobiles dashing by, suggested a picture to Sloan as other scenes suggested, or might have suggested, pictures to him,—for instance, the drunken woman to whom the policeman was so stern when she offered him a drink from her brown bottle. He watched a prostitute in a torn wrapper covered with a raincoat, with a veil over her hair, waiting for a bootblack; and especially he liked to watch the Throbbing Fountain, as he called it, which was invariably surrounded with men, women and children. Sloan wrote about this in his diary, "The sensuous attraction of the spurts of water is strong unconsciously in everyone." It seemed to have a hypnotic property, this pulsing jetting fountain with its little personal rainbow gleaming and fading, coming and going in the sunlight on the spray.

Many of these incidents and scenes appeared in the paintings and etchings of Sloan, as all who knew his work were to remember, scenes of spring rain on fresh green trees, of dust storms near the square, of snow at dusk with lights on Twenty-third Street. Sloan loved the sight and the feeling of the snow beating in his face, as he loved the electric signs against the Western sky, the Third Avenue Elevated against an early evening sky and lights at all times seen through a fog. Few sights pleased him more than a lighted florist's shop window in the evening in the rain, or, for a different sensation, the crowd in a bank against the buff-and-gold walls and the glass-hooded gratings.* Sometimes he left the city for

* See, in Sloan's diary of 1908, the details he noted in a bank that he painted, from memory, later: "At the Greenwich Savings Bank today I was hit by the idea that it would make a good subject for

Long Island or New Jersey,—for instance, Bayonne where, on the shore, among rickety buildings and shacks, yachts were being overhauled for the coming summer. He studied the white piers against the dull water when the sun was low and the brightly lighted hulls of a few of the yachts; then he took the trolley to Bergen Point where boys and girls in their Sunday gear were playing in circus-blue or bright red swings. He found Staten Island South Beach quite to his liking, suggesting the Atlantic City of years before, less touched by the new inventions than Coney Island, and, going to an automobile race once, he observed "a girl full of figure in a tight white sweater" who was, he said, "as much of a show as the rest."

But how much, as Sloan put it, "I enjoyed through my eyes,"—for another instance, a fine diving girl who came out of the water with her wet skirt gleaming so that it looked like the skin of a water-snake. This was at a beach on the Sound, all rocks and bathers, a scene that Maurice Prendergast would have liked. Then, especially in the earlier years, he was often on the ferry, when "New York still awed an unacclimated Pennsylvanian" and the boat was "the first lap of the road home." He loved fogs over the city and dark skies

---

a picture . . . A great number there and each an interesting life. The old woman lifting her overskirts and carefully putting her bank book in a white bag suspended from her waist. The old fellow in workman's jumper, another hard-faced old rascal with a silver-headed cane growling about red tape—a miserly villain. Old woman in threadbare skirt and faded red shawl painfully writing her signature. The vast buff and gold interior of the bank, the glass hooded gratings about the counters where the clerks under electric lights handle the books and money."

with lowering clouds, as one might have guessed from the "Wake of the Ferry," a picture that was "perhaps evoked by some nostalgic yearning," as Sloan said, for Philadelphia.* Sloan painted two canvases with this name, the first one being damaged,—he had thrown a rocking-chair at it in disgust;† and in painting them he was perhaps influenced by Whistler, who had also been by turns a painter and an etcher.

These city pictures were painted from memory, "from the realized thing seen in the mind," so that they were "more real," Sloan said, "than the things look,"—for "when the thing is in front of you, you may be confused by too much visual information." ‡ He worked as the Dutch genre painters had worked, never out of doors, making a hasty sketch of trees or boats, then running home to spend a fortnight finishing the picture for which the sketch served only as a reminder. Sloan would draw a few lines on the back of an envelope and later return to the spot, not to do any more drawing but to "soak it up," to study the character of the scene, the quality of the light there and what he called the "colour mood." Working in a low key, content with a lim-

* Writing of the New Jersey ferry, Sloan noted many years later, "Optimistic people go to the front of the boat, the depressed stand in the stern."

† Unlike Glackens, who sometimes threw his palette and brushes across the room, Sloan rarely indulged in tantrums while at his work.

‡ "The eyes don't see reality. They see colour pictures which are turned into reality by the mind . . . Realization is making the thing approach the reality of the thing seen in the mind . . . Two eyes can give you two views of the object, but only in the mind is the thing-concept created."

This explains Sloan's other remark, "A good picture should tell you some of the things a blind man knows about the world."

ited range of colours, black, blue, light red and yellow ochre, —following in this the taste of Eakins and Henri,—he worked in the teeth of what he called the "eyesight painting" of the Impressionists, with their orange lights, purple shadows, blues and pinks. For him grey was the city's prevailing tone; he found at least twelve distinct greys in it; and he supposed he was following the tradition of Velasquez, Frans Hals, Goya and Manet, using the "safe colours" that his own master loved. "It took years of experience with set palettes before I began to feel free to use the whole palette," he said later, when he no longer felt the "danger of losing one's place" by failing to follow those whom he took for his mentors.

CHAPTER VI

# THE EIGHT

One evening in 1907, Sloan, after dining with Henri, noted that they were both highly excited "over the possible venture into a gallery of the 'crowd,' our crowd." He was referring to Luks, Shinn, Glackens and themselves, the nucleus of "The Eight," so called, or to be called so presently when they exhibited in February of the following year. For Henri chose three other artists to be members of the group, Arthur B. Davies, Ernest Lawson and Maurice Prendergast, the Boston painter who was not yet living in New York.

What was the occasion for this group movement and why did it make such a stir and leave such a mark in the history of American painting, so that various critics, even then, and others later were to say that it founded the first American school of art? Henri was in revolt against the control of the art of the country by the National Academy of Design, and when this rejected in 1907 a painting by George Luks he declared that its jury system was obstructive and evil. Then, serving himself on the jury,—for he was a member of the Academy, as Glackens was already an associate member,— he withdrew two of his own paintings, one of them the "Gypsy Mother and Child," because the other jurors gave him second place. Henri, who had long since received academic honours not only in St. Louis and Pittsburgh but also in Paris, felt that these jurors insulted him in passing his work over in favour of their own work and the work of their friends. This was too much for the loyal John Sloan as well. Who were these men who presumed to put Henri in his place?

But this was only the last straw that broke the patience of the younger men who were waiting for some such incident to crystallize their minds. A new generation had come to the front that could not contain its resentment against this high-handed control of the world of art, the domination of the National Academy* over dealers and exhibition rooms,† over purchases by museums and the granting of scholarships and prizes. There were few outlets and fewer rewards for artists with something new to say who were bored by what Sloan called "the labours of K. Kox," by models posed in period costumes, young ladies draped in cheesecloth and what were described at the moment as "ideal nudes." Then there were the surface effects of the Impressionist artists who were still regarded as the last word of the modern. Academic painting

* "The National Academy is no more national than the National Biscuit Company," Sloan wrote with characteristic acidity in one of his notes.

† Of the galleries of the New York dealers before 1907, Guy Pène du Bois observed that they "vied in coldness and aloofness with the museums. They were hung in horrible red velvet and a pall of stuffy silence. One was invariably attended in them by an excessively well-mannered gentleman in afternoon clothes who seemed incapable of looking straight at anything without looking down his nose. Art was unquestionably designed for the captivation of tycoons, and everyone else was an intruder."—Du Bois, *Artists Say the Silliest Things*.

for Sloan was a matter of duplicating visual facts, a "minor job that the camera has taken over," and the school of the National Academy, as he put it, was "a place where you checked your brain at the door." He spoke for those who did not like the "blight of imitation," who did not want their pictures to be "sifted through the beards of the academicians" who formed the jury, and who were prepared, with Boardman Robinson, for a "battle between sterile minds and forms" and "blood-fed forms and living ideas." Along with Luks, the Academy rejected Sloan himself, Glackens and many another who disliked its mainly derivative eclectic art, —an art that was vaguely cosmopolitan and generally anæmic,—and who favoured, with Henri and the rest of their circle, a more or less native art that could fairly be described as independent. Not that they were nationalistic or conscious of any intention to glorify or even record the American scene, a phrase that Sloan always resented himself because of its nationalistic twist, resenting it more and more as time went on.* "American" did not mean to him that art should be patriotic, or limited to American subjects only, or that American artists should not study in Paris and paint Venetian scenes and Belgian girls. It was true that if he and his friends had set out to create an American art, they would

* "I am not for the American scene, I am for mental realization. If you are American and work, your work will be American."—John Sloan, *Gist of Art.*

"The American Scene, I resent the expression . . . Some of us used to paint little rather sensitive comments about the life around us. We didn't know it was the American Scene. I don't like the name . . . You can't open your eyes without seeing it, unless you are in an art gallery . . . A symptom of nationalism, which has caused a great deal of trouble in this world."—One of Sloan's later notes.

only have been doing what Europeans wanted, for invariably foreigners complained in New York that they found nothing American there and only what they already knew in Europe. But Sloan's sole motive, like that of his friends, was that "we loved life and people and tried to express that love of life,"—which happened to be American, both the life and the people; and "on that basis," he went on to say, "Prendergast, Lawson and Davies belonged with us."

Such was the origin of the "Eight," whom the dealer Macbeth exhibited on February 3rd, 1908, when three hundred people every hour crowded the rooms day after day and Davies said the event would mark an epoch.* For its success would result in more "group" exhibitions and destroy the prestige of the Academy in the end, he thought. Shinn sent Sloan a postcard he had had lithographed showing a procession of sandwich-men carrying up Fifth Avenue the pictures of the "Eight"; but their wine needed no such bush, especially as the exhibition was presently sent on to many other cities. It appeared in Philadelphia, Chicago, Detroit, Toledo, Indianapolis and Pittsburgh, while, on the opening night, the crowd gathered for dinner at Mouquin's and went on to a party at James Preston's. It was clearly apparent that Glackens had had too much to drink, Sloan wrote in his diary the following day, and "dear old Maurice Prendergast lost track of things." Prendergast, from Sloan's point of view, was "an overlooked painter of the highest order," some of

* Two years later, in 1910, Sloan wrote in his diary, "Stopping at Macbeth's, where I saw a very pretty comedy, Mr. Macbeth showing paintings to a prospective buyer. I told ——— that I should perhaps make a picture of the scene." This was the origin of his etching "The Picture Buyer."

whose personal memories resembled his own, for he too had painted show-cards and poster-advertisements in Boston and he had also illustrated books. He and his brother Charles carved picture-frames for Mrs. Jack Gardner, but the two were soon to come to New York to live. There was no market in Boston for Prendergast pictures. Sargent, at the moment, was the favourite there.

The date, 1908, was to be remembered all the more clearly because in that year also Alfred Stieglitz opened his "291" Fifth Avenue rooms, exhibiting, for the first time in America, the work of the new Paris schools and rivalling the show of the "Eight" as a symbol of rebellion. Otherwise, save for its after-effects, Henri's revolt might have been seen as merely one of a series of similar eruptions, Chase's in 1877, which created the Society of American Artists, or the revolt of the "Ten" in 1898. In this Childe Hassam and J. Alden Weir had protested against the stagnancy of the New York art world. But the "Eight" had a long train of consequences, for it led directly to the first Independent no-jury show of 1910 and later to the Society of Independent Artists. Moreover, it prepared the ground for the Armory Show of 1913, the nucleus of which was formed by the very same painters. Meanwhile, the "Eight" were first so called by Frederick James Gregg of the *Evening Sun,* a Dublin intellectual, a school friend of William Butler Yeats who had come to New York to live some years before. AE had once regarded the "prim and peremptory" Gregg,—as Sloan called him,—Ireland's hope in poetry, but, turning to prose, he rivalled as a brilliant journalist Charles Fitzgerald, his inseparable friend from Dublin who was also on the *Sun*. Between them, these two writers largely started the vogue of the "Eight" by giving them this name and extolling their work, interesting a multitude of newspaper readers in them, although the group had only one exhibition and were far too diverse in their talents to survive as a group. For while they were hailed as "New York realists," who were less realistic than Davies, Lawson and Maurice Prendergast? No members of the group were what Sloan called "long-hair flowing-tie" artists, nor yet were they "frock-coat high-hat" artists. But this did not make them brothers, even under the skin. Lawson was really idyllic, like Prendergast and Davies. A Scotsman of few words, born in San Francisco, a landscape painter who had studied with both Weir and Twachtman,—and also for a while at Julien's in Paris,—Lawson was a New York painter in that his work was mostly produced near the Hudson and Harlem rivers in upper Manhattan. But, like Twachtman, he was an Impressionist pure and simple.

Remote as they were from the rest of the circle, these three idyllic painters were all good friends of Sloan, who admired them greatly, though he hotly disputed Lawson's contention that Henri, by teaching, hurt his own work and that he wanted "to teach everybody." Sloan, for whom there were no spots on the sun of Henri, said that his master could benefit every other painter and that he was the greatest in all the American school, adding in his diary that he hated "this tendency of smaller men and women to yap at Henri." As for Davies, Sloan shared the general feeling at the time that he was a "poet" and "wonderful in his mastery of colour," observing, "I feel like an infant in colour compared with him" and his pictures "are beautiful even though you do not grasp their meaning." Again, Sloan wrote in his diary, "His work is like music" and "Arthur B. Davies is certainly a great man." * Yet what could have been further from Sloan's own work than Davies's visionary pastoral scenes of giant redwood glades and lakes in the Sierras, with figures from Greek mythology wandering round them, except perhaps Prendergast's fantasies, so wholly uninfluenced by Cézanne, whom he was the first American artist to discover? "You should know Cézanne!" Prendergast shouted, deaf as he was,—this was almost a refrain with the old Boston painter; for none of the other members of the "Eight," except Henri, knew Cézanne's work, although several were influenced by it a few years later. They had grown up as more or less "instinctive" painters.

In after years, Sloan, looking back, referred to the work of most of the "Eight" as "charming examples of the American realist school," words that no one used at the time about this "outlaw salon" that stirred up such a furore in 1908. What had the shouting been about, many a critic asked later when every eye was accustomed to the kind of things which the painters of the "Eight" originated, the "everyday subject-matter" that Sloan mentioned in his diary and that was so "unfamiliar then." The phrase "the Ash-can School" did not become current till the middle thirties, although Art Young had uttered it in 1916, expressing his dislike for a kind of picture in which ash-cans figured but without value for Socialist propaganda. Young used the phrase during a

* "Arthur B. Davies was rather an aloof kind of man, lived a sort of recluse's life . . . For Davies art was very much a thing inside the veil of the temple."—One of Sloan's notes, 1947.

quarrel at a board meeting of the *Masses*. But phrases like "the Black Gang" were bandied about at the time, or the "Black Revolutionists," referring to the difference between their dark work and the bright Impressionist pictures; and one critic asked, "Is it fine art to exhibit our sores?" as if Hogarth and Teniers had never painted.

As enemies of what passed for sweetness and light, the "Eight" were defenders of the ugly for those who were enamoured of Chase's "brush-work" and for whom "technique" was the sole end of art, and they were regarded as perhaps revolutionaries, in life as well as in art, who constituted a menace to the social order. Painting pigs with George Luks, or with Glackens dirty faces and the ragamuffin children near Washington Square,—dance-halls, dives, alleyways, night-courts, docks and gutters—was supposed in some fashion to discredit art. Or painting the scenes in the poor gaslit bedrooms that Sloan had watched across the way in his night-vigils at the window in West Twenty-third Street. It would have been useless to reply that Rembrandt had got more inspiration out of a dead bullock hanging in a butcher-shop than others had got from vistas of Bruges or Venice,—the "Prince of Darkness," Rembrandt,* who had pictured ruffians and vagabonds and old women making pancakes and paring their nails. What had Sloan done on

* Of all the world's artists, Rembrandt was perhaps the one whom Sloan admired most, early and late. In a speech at the Art Students' League in 1949, he spoke of Rembrandt's "simon-pure realism—more real than nature . . . He could paint a hand more real than the hand itself. If you want to prove it, try putting your hand against one that he has painted and shutting one eye. Your hand becomes flat, but the Rembrandt hand still has all three dimensions."

Sixth Avenue that Rembrandt had not previously done in the Ghetto and back lanes of Amsterdam, Sloan who had pictured "all the world . . . work, play, love, sorrow, vanity, the schoolgirl, the old mother, the harlot, the truant and the thief"? (For so he summed up these types in an interview later.) Or, for that matter, Luks, with his old woman curling her hair, his own Sixth Avenue beggars and "Matches Mary"? These realists were merely carrying out Emerson's injunction regarding the "milk in the pan" and the "meal in the firkin," the flat and the dull *to* the flat and dull that rest on the same foundations of wonder as the Parthenon or the towns of Athens and Troy. They were eschewing what Emerson had called "the sere remains of foreign harvests," carrying out Howells's counsel to work with the life they knew best and, by so doing, make "a new day in American art." For that matter, had not Mount and Eastman Johnson, like Eakins and Winslow Homer, done just this?—a fact that was overlooked in the uproar which the "Eight" aroused when the phrase the "American scene" was not yet a cliché. This fact was remembered in later days when Hopper and Benton followed the "Eight," with Burchfield, Reginald Marsh and so many others.

Sloan hated the phrase "the Ash-can School,"—and "now," he wrote later, "they have a new one . . . They call it the Journalistic Revolution," although there was nothing new in this, for Daumier and Constantin Guys had also been called outsiders in the world of art. They too had worked for newspapers, a fact that damned them in certain eyes, while they had presently found illustrious defenders, and Sloan, Luks, Glackens and Everett Shinn soon had admirers of influence too, especially Luks who appealed to the imagination of writers. James Huneker wrote two essays on the "swift brutal" Luks, with his Rabelaisian energies, so prodigal, so fecund, lacking repose and finish, to be sure, but such a believer in life and the beauty that is characteristic of it. He was a lover of "the familiar, the homely, the simple," with affinities that were Dutch rather than French, for whom the East Side was a happy hunting ground and who was full to the brim of New York life. How enlivening were Luks's biblical heads, his Gorky-like shoppers buying fish, his barrel-organs and children waltzing in the streets. Sloan, whose vogue had not begun,—if one could say that he had a vogue, either at that time or at any time later,—was pleased by Huneker's remarks on Luks, "a beautiful example of Huneker's ability to *interest* in art criticism. He's different," Sloan continued, "from the average critic in that they usually think they are sent by God to shield mankind from what they don't care for themselves." Luks appealed generally to literary men, he was so tangible and picturesque, and they wrote at length about his gusto, while, as for himself, Sloan seemed to take pleasure in antagonizing the critics and turning them against him. Their "knowing stupidity" irritated Sloan, their way of pointing out line combinations and light and shade arrangements as the "charm" of a picture, as if the quality of charm deserved any respect. He called them "fashion experts," and once he said that, to make a living, "in case of a complete mental breakdown, I might fall back on Art Criticism."

As for Huneker, reviewing the show, he ridiculed the nonsense that flooded the yellow press about "outlaws" and "rebels"; but, as Edward Hopper later observed, the "pap-fed" public had been unprepared for this sudden assault on its prudish and sentimental notions. Yet these artists had only looked at New York and painted the life they knew there as the French artists had painted Paris, exploring it in the spirit of Gavarni, for example, with Daumier's or Guys's relish for its character and life. Or, for that matter, Van Gogh's, who had gone into the streets and fields and caught the people in their everyday occupations. This was at a time, moreover, when New York did not seem "picturesque," as it seemed to a later generation, Sloan once noted, when ferry-boats and elevated railways became almost as romantic as Breton fishing-villages and Barbizon forests. For the rest, one could only have added that Glackens and Everett Shinn, at least, had seen New York rather in the light of Paris, which they tried to revisualize in their own city and which seemed to them less sordid and more vivacious. Touched as they were with the current belief that the adoption of French habits of mind was as indispensable for an artist as the experience of Paris, they retained an exotic flavour, which lingered in their work, though one sometimes found New York ash-cans in a corner of their pictures. Like Luks, who followed Frans Hals, they seemed clearly derivative, unlike Sloan, who was influenced by France at second-hand, if at all, while Glackens and Shinn almost always reflected French painters. Glackens and Shinn especially were cursed by a tendency to imitate other men. Sloan, less adroit than the others, was more authentic. Suspicious as he had always been of the technical facility of Chase, for instance, feeling a certain emptiness behind it, he had himself no cleverness of brush-work or of hand; and, never having seen Paris, he saw New York more in its own light than any of the others. His work, in its humanity and vitality, was all of a piece, expressing a consistent personal character and vision.*

Brief as the association was and casual in its grouping, the "Eight" made, nevertheless, a collective impression, although only seven pictures were sold, none of them by Sloan, who was never, he said, to "slip on contemporary success." But Sloan played a lone hand,—"I have always been a maverick," he said, "and always out of line with other people," never a yea-sayer without qualifications and never a whole-hearted member of any group except "the gang around Henri." He was too immersed in his work, he said, to make many friends, and he was sincere in adding, "Prizes have always been the least of my worries," while he worried still less over the question of selling his pictures. "What hope is there for Luks and Henri and other good work?" he asked himself. "The wonder is that such men have been produced from the loins of this age in America"; but for himself he was quite content that "puzzle work," even for years to come, remained his only regular source of income. Nor was he ever tempted to take up any "line,"—portrait or landscape painting,—that might have made money. The only pictures he painted for money were portraits that were commissioned, and he painted in sixty years only four

* "Of the older men, none seemed to me to equal John Sloan, who is essentially the painter of the low life of Victorian downtown New York. Sloan is a vigorous scintillating realist, who prefers low silvery tones, a master of atmosphere and gesture . . . a fuller-blooded, less capricious, less sardonic Sickert."—John Rothenstein, in *Horizon,* June, 1941.

of these, noting that even Henri refused to do the five o'clock tea-drinking that was necessary for portrait work in this country today. "If there is anything I despise it is these mouse-trap portrait-painters" who "entice sitters," he said, praising their dresses; and he might have reassured himself with the example of Winslow Homer, who remained perforce an illustrator for seventeen years. Winslow Homer had told a friend he would be content if he could be assured of a store salesman's income from his paintings; but Sloan, who made later a similar statement, required no reassurance, for he thought of contemporary success as artistic failure. "I am not so much interested in the man who is paid to paint," he said, "as I am in the man who pays to paint"; and he was willing to pay for his privilege because he believed that "an artist is an artist because he wants to live his own life."

## CHAPTER VII

# SOCIALISM: *THE MASSES*

WIDE AWAKE as John Sloan was to every phase of the life of New York, he had dropped in at the police courts now and then,—those haunts of Daumier and Gavarni once in Paris,—and, after visiting the Tombs Court and being shown through the prison, he watched the Harry Thaw trial in 1907. He spent at least one evening reading the detailed testimony, interested in the artist's-model chorus-girl wife, already so notorious as Evelyn Nesbit; and, seeing in Thaw's mother on the witness-stand a "fine old lady," he was disgusted with the prosecutor, William Travers Jerome. It struck him that this American uncle of the English Winston Churchill was playing to the reporters all the time, while, if he was a "sham," what could one say at the Jefferson Market night-court of the magistrates who administered snap justice there? Sloan, to whom one of his friends had been expounding socialism, began to feel there must be something in it as he watched the wretched women of the street,—types he was drawing for *Everybody's*,—subjected to the petty tyranny of the court-room. "My heart," he wrote, "melted one moment and grew red hot the next." For tragedy and comedy alike, he felt, there was more in two hours of the night-court than one could find in any but the greatest of plays.

As a young man in Philadelphia, Sloan had noted in a perfunctory way the Homestead Strike of 1892, the Great Northern strike and the gaoling of Debs for contempt, but, reading Ruskin, he had not been moved by this great writer's socialism and had paid little attention to economic questions. He and his friends, he said, had been "snobs about labour," and only the "cancerous growth" of the Republican party had caused him in 1896 to vote for Bryan. Henri had told him about Bakunin, but he had not read this writer and did not read him indeed for many years; for Henri was a consistent believer in philosophic anarchism who was to teach in the Ferrer School in New York.* Henri was a follower of Emma Goldman, and Sloan himself was "greatly impressed by her bravery and clear thought" when he heard her lecture on Mary Wollstonecraft. She struck him as "a great woman . . . hounded by the police for years . . . small, stocky, strong, almost handsome," who "did a lot to bring cultural ideas to Jewish working girls," for all her "platitudes of the propaganda." But, in spite of this and although Henri painted a portrait of Emma Goldman, and Dolly worked to raise bail for her on one occasion, Sloan never really liked her, in part because he had become too deeply concerned with socialism. So, while, in the interest of birth-control, he was ready to welcome her home from prison at a great mass-meeting later in Carnegie Hall, he could not go along the road with her. "She seems as an anarchist," he wrote, "to have few differences from the socialist but I suppose those few differences are of great

* Sloan noted that, in her autobiography, Emma Goldman told an untruth when she said he had taught with Henri at the Ferrer School.

importance," and he added, "Idealistic anarchists are people who look at a ladder and want the top rung without working their way up." It was the first rungs of the ladder that interested him. Sloan had formerly said, "I am of no party. I'm for the operating knife when a party rots in power." But now, abandoning his prejudices against organizations, he became an active member of the Socialist party.

For a few years, in fact, beginning in 1908, Sloan's diary bristled with notes on his connection with the party. On the Socialist ticket he ran for the Assembly in 1908 and six years later for a judgeship, remarking to a Better Government committee that asked what his qualifications were, "I think I know the difference between law and justice." But his other remark that he was "glad to lose" was a large understatement, for what would have become of the artist if he had won the election? However, he introduced speakers at socialist street meetings,—on one occasion in Wall Street at the corner of Broad,—he "spouted" socialism, as he said, against "the Plutocracy's government" and drew cartoons for the *Call,* which he read every day. In Madison Square he left on the benches copies of the *Appeal to Reason,* "in the fond hope of spoiling someone's peace of mind"; and, trying to convert "Mr. T." and "bring him over to the 'only way,' " he tried also to convert a carter who was delivering pictures. But in this man there was no revolt, he was of the contented sort with "a little home of his own" and all the rest, though Sloan could not comprehend why it was the workers did not vote *en masse* for socialism. He himself went to business meetings at the Rand School at which I.W.W. speakers appeared from the Far West and Charles Edward Russell

MY WIFE IN BLUE (DOLLY), 1917

JOHN SLOAN, 1906

*Portrait by Robert Henri*

defended freedom of speech; and he dined at "Comrade" Morris Hillquit's with Art Young and Ernest Poole for whose stories he was drawing pictures in the *Saturday Evening Post.* Delighting in Art Young's "splendid things," he admired this "man of interesting character" whose work he regarded as "strong, simple, direct,"—he always called Art Young "our best cartoonist,"—and he was ready himself when the comrades asked him for drawings for the Rand School exhibition. He referred in his diary to "that great socialist Jesus Christ . . . a Revolutionist,"—given as he was to those terrible simplifications that spring from overheated minds and deep as he was in Oscar Wilde's *The Soul of Man under Socialism,* in Jack London's *Martin Eden* and Gorky's tales. These stories explained "some great part of the fearful conditions," he wrote, "in the whole present social system," conditions that seemed much the same in America as in Russia.

While many, perhaps most, of his artist friends were on the left politically, Sloan could not convert Glackens to socialism, for Glackens, with all his "good solid stuff," would not listen to his arguments any more than the impenitent Everett Shinn. Nor would his old master the anarchist Robert Henri. As for Rollin Kirby, he was "foetid with conservatism," and, scolding Sloan for his socialist obsession, he was unable to see how any artist could be interested in it. He said it had cost Sloan his sense of humour, and so seriously did the two take this bone of contention that the result was virtually a broken friendship. Even Jerome Myers found his company uncongenial when Sloan became convinced of socialism, for this brother of the author of the *History of the*

*Great American Fortunes* preferred the idea of an aristocratic system. Sloan was fond of Jerome Myers and his "pleasant . . . soothing way" and felt that he should have been a member of the "Eight," of which he was only not a member because he was too much of Henri's age to adopt the position of disciple that Henri demanded. Another Philadelphian, he had come to New York in 1886 and painted scenery for the theatres there; then, loving summer in the city, like Sloan, he had loved especially the lower East Side, the push-carts, the bums on park benches, the organ-grinders. Sloan had walked the streets with him through dingy heaps of melting snow with children swarming in the pools over slushy mounds, with the curb vegetable markets, the blue looking chickens and the meat-wagons in the mud under the sun. Myers, a pessimist, was even to oppose the idea of the Independent Artists, for he thought there were too many artists already; but Sloan met his brother Gustavus Myers at the Rand School with Big Bill Haywood, the "one-eyed kind-faced" man.

Another socialist was Rockwell Kent, who seemed to Sloan at first "a fine energetic character and a big painter . . . an eager man, eager for life, eager in his ideas" and "a good out and out revolutionist" also. His pictures of great rocks and a winter sea struck Sloan as "like big prayers to God" which he accepted as great and enjoyed to the utmost; and Kent, a lover of northern coasts, urged Sloan to join him on a late-autumn voyage to Newfoundland. He had even thought of starting an art colony there, and from North Sydney he wrote to Sloan, "You should have heard me planting discontent in the minds of the miners." He had found the ocean grand and stormy, and, changing his personality from that of a cultured young tourist, he played the part of a rough type of workingman. Seated with the immigrants about the festive oil-clothed board, he had half a mind to join them in the coal-mines, seven hundred feet underground, two or three miles from the foot of the shafts,—what a wonderful experience that would have been! He painted a satin pillow-case for the hotel-keeper's daughter and got $1.50 for the job; and Sloan said he "created excitement among simple folk, business men and bankers," * by freely airing his views on his return. He rented a studio in Sloan's building in West Twenty-third Street. In time Sloan's feeling for Kent grew decidedly cooler.

In his socialist activities, Sloan was abetted, and more than abetted, by his wife, the tiny, devoted, bellicose, emotional Dolly, for, while he was by nature an introvert and somewhat passive in practical affairs, she was well known as a "hustler" in the Socialist party. Sloan said he felt like a shirker once in comparison with his "Frankenstein," the name he gave to one of his socialist converts, and he had no great liking for parades or meetings, while Dolly, "the little wonder woman," was always "on the Socialist firing line." She was in her element distributing tracts and selling books at meetings in the streets, marching in suffrage processions, working for causes,—pacifism, socialist picnics, birth control,—and she was responsible more or less for the hiring of

* About business men in general, Sloan shared a feeling that was common in his time among American artists. In a lecture in 1932, he said, "Business men are peddlers on a large or small scale. They buy something for five cents and sell it for eight or ten, except in Santa Fé, where they sell it for thirty. That's what a business man is."

Madison Square Garden once and crowding the vast hall with listeners who paid to get in. Always "down" or "up" herself, and something of an exhibitionist, she almost required a cause to pull her together, a cause that enabled her to feel she was "marching towards victory" with the rest of the crowd, raising money for Tom Mooney's attorneys or Emma Goldman's bail. Or collecting a fund for strikers or working for the recognition of Ireland at the Peace Conference after the first world war. Like none of the other socialists, she could get along with the Irish police, who saw that she was Irish and politically minded and who liked her because she was so diminutive also. She never had any trouble dealing with them, and this made her a great success in running street meetings. She even tried to make socialists out of the policemen. Ernest Poole remembered later the meeting in Carnegie Hall in behalf of Arturo Giovannitti when two Italian reds were ramping at the rear to come out and call on the boys to throw the sheriff and his deputies off the platform. Of these there were no less than thirty, stalwarts every one, and of course a riot was just what the sheriff hoped for. But suddenly, in her red dress, Dolly appeared on the stage and passed the collection plate along the line of policemen. A roar of laughter arose from the hall. Once again Dolly had saved the day.

Sloan himself was always praising the "brave little woman,"—"I feel proud of the way she is rising to the work," he wrote after a street meeting in 1910; and she said that Sloan was only a better socialist than herself because he had her to deal with the grocer. But the secret of it all was that, having no "ideologies," she "cared for people,"

Sloan said after her death. "She had no intellectual interest or understanding of social theories . . . Through me she came into contact with socialism. Under other circumstances she might have put the same sympathy and hard work behind Tammany, anywhere that she felt people would be helped"; and, while Sloan himself was far more complex, his socialism was not theoretical either but sprang from a similar fount of human compassion. He never read a word of Marx, he said on one occasion, but often in his journal he noted some pitiful scene that evoked in him the desire to "do something" about it,* and when he turned down a poor rum-soaked bum who asked him for money he would shrink home feeling, as he said, "below cost." While these notes were usually uncoloured by any second thought, they were still indications of the passion for justice that Sloan shared with Goya, the "painter of humanity" in Spain, a passion that for many of the best minds of the time embodied itself in socialism, with its will to right the miseries and wrongs of the world. For Sloan the movement was symbolized in the dedicated figure of Eugene V. Debs, the tall gaunt Abraham Lincoln-like man who appealed deeply to Sloan and who stood for a similar indifference to the doctrinaire.†

* E.g., "Walked today, and at a distance shadowed a poor wretch of a woman on Fourteenth Street. Watched her stop to look at billboards, go into Five Cent stores, take candy, nearly run over at Fifth Avenue, dazed and always trying to arrange hair and hatpins. To the Union Square lavatory. Then she sits down, gets a newspaper, always uneasy, probably no drink as yet this day. My study is interrupted by Davis," etc.—May 24th, 1907.

† "After Debs died," Sloan wrote once, "I never kept myself strictly to the Socialist ticket when voting."

For, thinking socialism "right in the main," Sloan said he was "rather more interested" in human beings than in schemes for betterment, and he even asked himself at times if they would be so interesting when they were all comfortable and happy. He lost much of his faith in political action when the socialist parties went to pieces in Germany and France in 1914, and he dropped his membership in the party whose theories had never stirred his mind, though in feeling he remained a socialist to the end of his life.* Without caring for party politics, he deeply believed in the idea that the public utilities of the country, and its natural resources, should not be held by the few for their own profit; but, having no rigid tenets, he was always an independent, even when he was an actual member of the party. He believed profoundly in human nature, which so many regarded as evil, convinced that "the good gods were invented" to express the inner craving for the good in man, convinced as well that it was wrong to say you can't change human nature

---

When, for opposing the first world war, Debs was imprisoned he kept on the wall of his cell in Leavenworth Sloan's drawing, "A Medal and Maybe a Job." Representing a wounded soldier crawling along the ground and reaching up to receive a medal, this was the only anti-war drawing that Sloan ever made (in August, 1914).

* "I have fond hopes for the progress of socialism in England," he wrote in 1951.

In 1948 Sloan joined the Progressive Citizens of America to promote the candidacy of Wallace, but he felt that Wallace was "not sufficiently astute as a politician." Besides, he soon recognized that Wallace's case was hopeless "because the Communists gave him the 'kiss of death.'"

Voting for Truman, he said, "The socialist Norman Thomas would be best but has no chance, unfortunately. Lord protect us from Dewey and Republicans."

since evidently poverty and ignorance were holding back its growth. He described as "all rot" the opinion of an editor who said that millions of readers were not educated up to John Sloan's etchings, remarking, "The reason that it's hard to reach the 'common' people is that educated idiots in droves block the path, protecting them . . . The people have always taken the best that has been offered." Believing in socialism through the vote, through the conviction of the majority, he was opposed to socialism *as a religion,** the Communist form that was taking a leaf out of the Roman Catholic book, establishing a "religious system with saints and inquisitions." A humanist in grain and bone, he distrusted Russia as time went on for using in politics the symbolism and methods of religion, although, as with many old socialists, it never made him happy to hear of the failure of the socialist state in Russia.† He was convinced that the lust for money had merely been replaced there by the lust for power over other people, and he had no use for the Communists who, already in 1910, were doing their best to break up socialist meetings. He piqued a group of them when he said once that he would like to see them take over the country "because then we would be rid of Communists." He especially detested people who got on the "radical band-

* John Sloan did not like the idea of art *as a religion* either. In his diary, 1908, he wrote, "B. speaks of a man being *religiously* interested in his work. This may mean well but does not sound 'healthy' to me."

† Sloan was one of three Americans who were invited to attend the Soviet International Congress of Revolutionary artists at Moscow, 1933. All expenses were to be paid, including the expense of a tour of the Soviet Union. Sloan had no interest in attending this, although he was pleased to be invited, and later he said he did not remember answering the invitation.

wagon" because they wanted power over others. But because for him it was a philosophy, not a religion, Sloan never lost his faith in socialism, differing in this from many of the Communists themselves. As William Ellery Channing said, "No one is so inclined to believe too little as the one who began by believing too much." *

It was at the height of his radical phase that Sloan joined the *Masses*, the weekly founded by Piet Vlag, a socialist of the Rand School, that became generally known in 1912.† Max Eastman took it over then, with Floyd Dell, John Reed and others through whom it became famous in the world of art and letters, largely because of its illustrations, contributed by sixty artists or so, among them Art Young, Glenn O. Coleman and Stuart Davis. Sloan, who had bought ten street-life prints of Glenn O. Coleman's drawings, greatly admired Boardman Robinson, another of the artists, regarding him as "a master of creative graphic design," but he had many reservations about still another, George Bellows, Henri's "arrived" pupil who had come from Ohio. Connected with the Association for Improving the Condition of the Poor, Robinson had seen much of the impoverished and disheartened, and his experience had made a socialist of him; and Bellows had become a socialist too, though he sometimes threatened to leave the *Masses* and join Emma Gold-

* Sloan wrote later, in 1928, "I am still a socialist in my ideals but have had no hope of *political* socialist results since 1914." He had come to agree with Debs when he said, "We socialists aren't going to get it. It's coming out of the natural evolution of society."

† Earlier, in 1909, Sloan had discussed with the city editor of the *Call* the idea of starting a humorous socialist paper along the lines of *Simplicissimus*.

man's anarchist *Mother Earth.* A baseball player in his native state who had been offered a professional career, he continued to "play to the stands," Sloan always felt, though his brilliant and vigorous pictures were so much better than most, he said, that one was obliged to admire them nevertheless. Bellows was already established with his canvas "Sharkey's" in 1908, later to be followed by the "Dempsey-Firpo Fight," but even though Henri had "rocked him back on his heels," in Sloan's view, he "never got away from the Charles Dana Gibson" note.* Popular among sports reporters, he was well-known for his lithographs and, along with Rockwell Kent, Sloan instructed him in etching. Sloan was pleased with the policy of the *Masses,* which allowed almost as much space for the pictures as for the stories, articles and poems. The plans for its format and contents alike had been based on a study of *Le Rire* and *Punch, Jugend, Simplicissimus* and other papers and the work of Daumier, Steinlen, Charles Keene and Forain.

In two or three essays that were later reprinted in his *Journalism Versus Art,* Max Eastman explained this policy of the *Masses,* saying it was the only American illustrated magazine that habitually declined to conciliate its readers. "It never considered its advertisers or its subscription list in deciding what art and what writing it was to publish," while

* Sloan never liked Bellows either as an artist or as a man. "Bellows, after all," he wrote, "was just a sentimental illustrator . . . As a painter he was a great ball-player, with his eye on the bleachers . . . You can see the feet of clay, maybe clay at both ends." Elsewhere Sloan said that Bellows had "no selective impulses" and that he was a "soda fountain with an inexhaustible supply of flavours, all except that of alcohol."

the effort of others "to please a great many people all the time" resulted "in a drab and mediocre semblance of art . . . The thought of a magazine cover makes me tired." How monotonous was the usual magazine art, Eastman went on to say, with its girls by Gibson and Christy and Harrison Fisher, artists who had "given up their profession of realizing in line the varieties of life and gone into the manufacturing business." * For the rest, in reply to a denunciation by the editor of *Collier's* of the "morality" of these new artists who so loved destitutes, prostitutes and "bad smells," Max Eastman said, "It is a queer morality which can escape the grip of the tragic problems of our time by turning the eye in another direction." With all this John Sloan, the art editor, heartily agreed. Later he said, "The *Masses* set a pace and had an influence on all periodicals after that. Certainly the *New Yorker* in a more sophisticated and less liberal way patterned itself on the early *Masses.*"

At the outset and for two or three years, Sloan was delighted with the *Masses,* of which Dolly was the business manager for a month or two, born organizer that she was and always working to find money for artists who could not pay

* "I can see Sloan, at a *Masses* meeting, holding up a drawing by Stuart Davis of two sad, homely girls from the slums of Hoboken, and proposing the title, 'Gee, Mag, think of us bein' on a magazine cover.' That formed our June cover, which was much commented on. It was realism; it was also revolt."—Max Eastman, *Enjoyment of Living.*

At a time when the Gibson girl was "the peak of inspiration" to students of illustration all over the country, Adolf Dehn said that "a great light broke" when Western students saw the *Masses* with its allegedly crude and vulgar pictures."—A. Christ-Janer, *Boardman Robinson.*

their rent.* Sloan contributed to the paper, without pay, first or last, fifty-three drawings, including covers. Like the *Call,* for which he also worked gratuitously during these years, if offered him "subjects of a human nature sort and good chances to make pictures . . . Just what is not true," he continued in his diary, "of most of the paid illustrations in the magazines." Even the new covers of the *Masses* were a real departure, and, in general, he wrote later, "We cut loose from a sort of tight type of illustration current at the time." On the night when the *Masses* first came out, he sold seventy-eight copies, more than all the other editors put together, approaching people at the suffrage parade and even jumping on their running-boards, telling them it was going to be worth "ten dollars some day." Later, when Max Eastman was absent, he took charge of two issues, sending for Eastman's approval a tiny model of the magazine with a parody of each of the drawings in miniature. Loving the *Masses,* Eastman said, "he would waste time on it in the same childish way I would," while he had "real executive ability," with good judgment and confidence in it, together with the "faculty of directed action." He knew all about make-up, printing and engraving. Art Young said that Sloan was "a man of universal vision and understanding."

But when propaganda became the central interest of the magazine and the editors seemed more concerned with orthodoxy than with drawings that showed a response to human life, Sloan felt it was not for him,—it was no longer "fun"; and in 1916 he resigned, with Glenn O. Coleman

* Dolly Sloan organized also Branch One of the Socialist party, the "highbrow" branch to which many intellectuals belonged, including Sinclair Lewis, Ernest Poole and William English Walling.

and Stuart Davis, who were equally opposed to the doctrinaire. Eastman, Floyd Dell and Art Young, who took over the direction and who were too political, from Sloan's point of view, were glad to be rid of him as not political enough, although Eastman had felt at first, as he wrote later, that he and Sloan had agreed better than any of the others. At the time he remarked that he enjoyed Sloan's wit and artistic genius but would also enjoy the "absence of his coöperation," while Art Young was not interested in any kind of work that did not have propaganda in it. There had been a perpetual feud between Sloan and himself regarding this, one that had led to constant quarrels, and Young had observed that "our side" thought we were contributing to the revolution "if we put an ash-can in a drawing." ("Our side" consisted of Sloan, Davis and Coleman, and this was the phrase that denominated the "Ash-can School.") Stuart Davis especially objected when the editors rewrote the captions to give them what they called a more "social" twist, and Sloan was convinced that the magazine could spread the socialist idea with more effect by retaining a freer outlook. It would have survived, he felt, the first world war period if it had not become involved in dogma. Its humorous perspective had meant everything to Sloan, who lost interest in it more and more after the war began and more and more the magazine followed ideological lines. He had also wished it to maintain its coöperative organization, in which all the editors voted on one another's work, while Eastman, who had to raise money and run it, knew that a magazine could only be run with an editor-in-chief who made decisions. "It just proves that real democracy doesn't work—yet," Sloan remarked after his resignation. Eastman was sorry that he could have no more of the flame and blood-coloured covers that Sloan had made at the time of the Colorado coal-strike, while, as for Sloan, he said of Eastman, whom he seldom saw in later years, that he had a great gift for pulling the magazine together.

For Sloan, all this was illuminating,—his connection with the *Masses* and political life,—but he was not the only one for whom, as for Emerson, politics "put confusion" in the brain. Socialism made him, he said, self-conscious and angry, it disturbed his "thinking as a painter," and moreover it subtly weaned him away from painting city pictures by giving him ulterior thoughts about his subject-matter. "It was interest in life and the poetic beauty of things seen when I moved about the city that made me want to paint pictures," Sloan wrote once. "Love of the people came into it—not what they call social consciousness now, the working man bulging with muscles (like peanuts) or bowed down under his burden (of overalls drawn like crushed tin cans)." * He said Emma Goldman demanded of the artist too much social consciousness, asking him to paint, for instance, a rich woman covered with diamonds in order to show that she was a parasite. This would take the picture "out of art—which is simple truth, as felt by the painter"; and, knowing that "innocence and simple affection for humanity" had dictated his best work, Sloan found that social consciousness got in his

* "The realism of the modern proletarian art is realism based on subject-matter and has not enough to do with realization. The realism of the 'Eight' is based on realization."—John Sloan in a radio interview, 1937.

Sloan, who disliked "anti-movements," said, "I believe that if I felt the social current inspired me, I would get out of the current. I'd think it was an undertow."

way. Whenever he felt himself involved in preaching socialism, he said, he could not see his way to painting a picture, adding, "This quirk may have kept me from painting a lot more city pictures,"—as, in point of fact, it unquestionably did. Referring to his "crisis of conscience" of the years 1909-1912, he said he was so concerned about socialism that he very seldom "saw pictures," and for two or three years he almost ceased to paint, for his purpose in painting was virtually paralyzed. He felt he had surrendered to the cause his own life as an artist, and when he returned to painting again he found he had outgrown his "city" phase and went in largely for landscape and figure painting. He made it a rule never to paint with the "propaganda content" that destroyed his innocent feeling about the city,* reserving this literary motive for his etching and presently for his drawings and cartoons alone. For the rest, he said there was "no democracy in art," and, always believing in democracy in economic and political matters, he knew that in cultural matters it was out of the question.† His final conclusion about painting was, "I don't believe an artist has any duty to society in his work."

* The only picture Sloan ever painted with conscious social intent was his "Recruiting, Union Square." In the square, in 1908, he had seen a United States Army recruiting sign with a soldier in attendance, and he noted that the tired bums on the benches still "stuck to the freedom of their poverty." Sloan, who was a pacifist, added, "There is a picture in this,—a drawing or etching probably." He ended by painting the scene but he remarked that he "felt self-conscious about it."

† Sloan said repeatedly, "It may be taken as an axiom that the majority is always wrong in cultural matters . . . Voting on matters of taste always results in selection of the mediocre or commonplace . . . Politically I believe in democracy, but culturally not at all . . . Whenever a cultural matter rolls up a majority I know it is wrong."

CHAPTER VIII

# AT PETITPAS': J. B. YEATS

IN THE COURSE of the summer of 1908, John Sloan fell in one day with the Irish painter and philosopher John Butler Yeats, known to many as the father of the poet but known to a devoted few as a man of extraordinary powers in his own right. Yeats, who had arrived in the United States a few months before this, presently settled at Petitpas' in West Twenty-ninth Street, a boarding-house kept by three sisters from Brittany where a number of artists and writers, journalists, actors and teachers gathered about him. "It is my belief," he wrote, "that Shelley, living in these days, would have preferred New York to Rome," and, having decided at the age of seventy that there was no future at home for him, he was to remain in New York for the rest of his life. He saw no reason why he should be an old man in a Dublin chimney-corner; and, chastening the Americans because he liked them, he singled out John and Dolly Sloan for a very special measure of his affection.

This "fine unspoiled old artist gentleman," as John Sloan called him once, had always been interested in the minds of artists, and he had not only watched painters and poets but he had instructed in his way the bright young people of his time in Dublin. All his four children were artists of one sort or another, and he had known most of the figures of the Irish "revival," of whom not a few were also living in New York, among them Padraic and Mary Colum and the founder of the Hermetic Society, Charles Johnston, the Sanskrit scholar, with his Russian wife. Johnston had been a school-friend of William Butler Yeats, like the Dubliners Frederick James Gregg and Charles Fitzgerald, those brilliant staff-writers of the *Evening Sun* who had come out strongly for the "Eight" and who often appeared at Petitpas' with the Johnstons. It was true that they preferred the more glamorous Mouquin's, the old red-plush French restaurant under the Sixth Avenue elevated railway that figured in the best-known of Glackens's paintings. Sometimes George Luks came to Petitpas' with Gregg and Fitzgerald, who were all adulation for this vigorous painter, though Luks sometimes behaved like a maundering fool when he had had too much to drink, bragging about Synge and "Bill" Yeats whom he had never seen. He became, for Sloan, "porcine," no longer picturesque. At Petitpas' one saw Glackens too, with Henri, the Prendergasts and Everett Shinn, and George Bellows's lithograph "Yeats at Petitpas'" commemorated an evening there when conversation finally gave place to dancing.* Three English actors were constant frequenters one of whom lived for a time with me in my lodging-house near "Death Avenue" on West Twenty-third Street,—for I came into the picture at Petitpas' also; and it was there that I first met John Sloan. Another frequenter was Jones, the American editor of the *Strand Magazine* who

* With his occasional second sight, J. B. Yeats said when he first saw George Bellows, "There is a man who is going to die early."

had toured the country as manager for Mrs. Langtry and who at the moment was writing Edison's life. There was also "Comrade" André Tridon, the Greenwich Village character who annoyed Sloan by saying that the Anglo-Saxon temper was "not delicate enough for pastels" and that Glackens's were "brutal"; and Joaquin Miller's daughter and Rockwell Kent were occasionally there with Horace Traubel, Whitman's Camden Boswell. J. B. Yeats asked him if Whitman believed in ghosts and fortune-telling, in which he had an unclouded faith himself, but the gentle kindly Traubel, as Sloan called this editor of the *Conservator,* found himself unable to answer the question.

To one visitor Yeats was especially drawn, the Harvard poet of whom Sloan wrote that he looked like Aubrey Beardsley but was rather too "priggish," although Yeats said that "every young poet talked that way,"—he knew, for he had himself "brought up a poet." Later he wrote to his son "Willie" that Alan Seeger, as a poet of the war, was "infinitely more interesting" than Rupert Brooke, and Seeger, whom Yeats liked to sketch, appeared in the conversation-piece that was ultimately one of John Sloan's most famous pictures.* He may have been one of a group of us,—three

* Regarding this picture, J. B. Yeats himself wrote, "It reminds me of Dickens. There is only one figure sympathetically rendered. It is that of Alan Seeger and was painted long before this war in which he was killed; on every other face is a smile which is wicked caricature. Seeger is sitting as I so often saw him, courteously attentive yet himself silent, his head drooping forward, all of him in deep shadow—a man with a poet's soul, of which there is ample evidence in what he has written—it is scarce among the writers of accomplished verse. It was characteristic of Sloan to introduce this note of tender appreciation into the noisy scene. One is tempted to think that he is psychic and knew what must happen."—*The Seven Arts,* April, 1917.

or four, I think,—whom Yeats took one day to lunch at "Quinn's," the tall bland courtly Irish-American lawyer art-patron of the time who bought a complete set of John Sloan's etchings. John Quinn, who kept Yeats supplied with cigars and came to his rescue financially, commissioning the self-portrait, for instance, that Yeats painted from a mirror, was loyal especially to Irish artists, among them Jack Yeats and AE, the painter who was akin, Sloan felt, to Arthur B. Davies. His rooms were crammed with works of art, paintings by Augustus John and sculptures of Gaudier-Brzeska, as I remember, for Quinn, like the Yeatses, had been greatly impressed by the critical views of Ezra Pound, who also came to Petitpas' on one or two occasions. Sloan had not yet read Pound's poems,—few had read them at that time, although they were influencing the poet Yeats* already,—but he was interested in Pound at once if only because he had spent some time as a student in Sloan's Philadelphia.

One evening Quinn took Sloan, Pound and Yeats, in a big touring-car—Sloan's first drive in one,—to Coney Island, where, after dining and talking till nearly ten o'clock, they all set out to see the shows. While Sloan rode on an elephant's back, one and all shot the chutes and even Yeats joined them in a wild ride in tubs, ready as he was for any

* Sloan seems to have met the poet Yeats only once. He noted in his diary for October 11th, 1911, the "great news that W. B. Yeats will be at Petitpas' tonight" and "J. B. Yeats wants me to be there to meet him." He continues, "About 8:45 'Willie' arrived," but Sloan felt "he had been lionized so much that he could not be natural." However, though he "did all the talking," he talked "interestingly." Sloan failed to record just what the poet said.

adventure, sharing Quinn's boyish enthusiasm for these New York sights which, however, were nothing new to Sloan. For during his first two New York years Sloan had visited Dreamland and Luna Park, wandering all over Coney Island, "trying to soak it up," he wrote, "like a blotter in a sea of variegated inks." Eating frankfurters, popcorn and peanuts, he had peeped into the concert-halls, amused by the gaudy bawdy beauties, listened to the talk of the fortune-tellers and the roars of natural vulgar mirth at the lingerie displays of the girls on the bamboo chute. Watching the people watching the surf, he had delighted above all in the sand-covered bathing-suits of the women on the beach, lolling and cavorting and yet like sandstone sculpture, and the beautiful tawdry magnificence of the night illuminations were only too picturesque for him. Feeling that there was a lot of fine material for pictures there, he also felt as he felt in Chinatown that for his purpose there was too much in the scene, for in Mott Street and Pell Street it seemed to him that the details of the life would be good for him if the Chinese themselves were "secondary interests." He had serious doubts about Coney Island as the right place for him, and when John Kraushaar* urged him to paint it, saying

* From 1916 onward, and long before it began to sell, the Kraushaar Galleries exhibited Sloan's work with devoted regularity. Sloan, who called John F. Kraushaar "the most honest art dealer in the country," had reason for praising his loyal faith as well. For he and Miss Antoinette Kraushaar, his daughter, who succeeded him, stood by Sloan whether his work sold or not. During many years the Kraushaar Galleries received no return for the cost of the Sloan exhibitions.

Sloan's etching "Kraushaar's," 1926, represents John Kraushaar "selling a picture," as Sloan wrote, "to a man whose wife feels she needs sables."

he would have a great success, he resolved never to see the place again. He wrote in his diary, "There is something of the mule in me."

This was an example of what Yeats called Sloan's "won't power," which he said was quite as marked as the will power of others, for, loving and admiring Sloan, Yeats found reasons now and then for teasing, scolding, reproving and admonishing him also. More than once he said of Sloan that of all the contemporary American artists he was the one whose work was most likely to last, and he was severe with Sloan because he respected him so much and wished to see him develop to the utmost of his powers. The two, or, rather, the three were soon constantly together, for Yeats was devoted to Dolly as well and was "all smiles" whenever they met, as Sloan remarked when their friendship was still new. He made several drawings of her in pastel or pencil, and he said of her that she had "no bravery,"—no ostentation, no parade,—but that she had "the courage of the devil." He was always observing and quoting her, how she talked of her "second husband" when what she was thinking of really, as he noted in a letter, was "John Sloan's second wife," and he encouraged her habit of going to soothsayers and palmists, a habit that was very like his own. At the same time, his faith in her, in her admirable qualities, strengthened her far from adequate self-esteem,* and, largely because of this feel-

* Speaking of Sloan's picture "A Woman's Work," Yeats said that we have here "the woman of the domestic imagination, peacable, rooted in the small activities of busy life, a woman to infuse tenderness and cure passion. We have evidence that the artist liked her best of all." This was a type that deeply appealed to Yeats himself, and he communicated his liking to Dolly, in whom he sometimes saw the type embodied.

ing of Yeats, she stopped commuting to Philadelphia to find a cure for her nerves and tensions there. For the rest, he often wrote to her saying how much he loved John Sloan, who was "so quick in response and so fiercely tender . . . I find in him such a rich and varied humanity." Elsewhere he spoke of "the depth and force of Sloan's affectionateness," together with "his genius in painting pictures," and he said to Dolly, "*Your* genius is action, that is why both are perennially interesting and lovable."

The friendship of the Sloans and Yeats, intimate almost from the start, remained to the end firm, complex and filial-paternal, and Sloan could scarcely contain his grief when Yeats died in 1922, still young after spending thirteen years in this country. Yeats, on the whole, had been happy here, finding in America "wells of feeling which easily become well-springs of desire and well-springs of ideality," he wrote in *Harper's Weekly,*—an "inspired hopefulness" that imparted to New York faces "the look of expectation and holiday." He added, in *The Seven Arts,* that he loved the summer of New York because of its splendour and pomp and its festiveness,—a feeling that he shared deeply with Sloan,—notwithstanding its dreadful heat, shattering to mind and body, and its swarming mosquitoes plaguing the tired crowds. Yeats formed the habit of dropping in, perhaps with his little satchel of chalks, to undertake another sketch of Dolly, always a welcome guest for both with his "steady warm shower of reminiscences and ideas and kindliness and good humour," Sloan recorded. Abstemious, he asked for nothing more than a little pea-soup and red wine,—or a glass of French Vermouth, which he liked above all, seldom drinking anything stronger, though he said his idea of perfect bliss was the second drink of Jameson's stabilized forever. He would relate his last night's dream or read a short story he had just composed or describe a play he was planning about a house that was haunted. He had dreamed of a bird killed by a cat,—a bad omen this would prove to be,—or he had dreamed of catching a very large fish, which he believed was a sign of good fortune for him; and, starting possibly a portrait group of the two Sloans together, he would read aloud a letter from his daughter Lily. She had had a remarkable dream about a white rose and a flame. Because of his faith in clairvoyance, Sloan bought for him Cheiro's book on palmistry, just the thing, he noted, to give "dear old Yeats." Discoursing on ghosts, a favourite theme, Yeats was a capital reader who was fond of reading Synge's plays aloud or his son's plays, *The Green Helmet,* for one, which he read, Sloan wrote, with "proud tears" in his eyes as he brought it to a finish. He read Gautier's essay on Paul Scarron to the Sloans, and he read a story of Edgar Allan Poe, delighting in Poe's poems too, many of which he had just discovered. He knew well, Sloan said, how to read the best parts and how to make them tell.

At the head of his table at Petitpas', Yeats was always very cross when, after dinner, his friends left "so soon," but there were times when he understood it, as, for instance, when he wrote to Dolly that he had been bored himself between two ladies. The "silly vociferation" of one made conversation impossible, and so did the "subtle antagonistic airs" of the other. Sloan noted a few of his remarks at table, about his experiences as a portrait painter, in the eighteen-seventies, in the house of the Irish Lord Herbert, repeating the Rabelaisian jokes and describing the visiting lady who, as Yeats remembered, threw herself at him. He added that he himself had been "too much awed to accept," aside from the fact that he had a wife and children. He told a story of a father who died and the children afterwards found his cane and exclaimed, "Mamma! Papa forgot his stick!"; and one day when he was very depressed because he had had no news from home Mrs. Charles Johnston relieved him by a reading of the cards. When one challenged his superstition, he supported it ably enough somewhat along the lines of Pascal's wager, "We don't know how much we don't know. Who knows?"—therefore, why should we not believe? Yeats was lecturing here and there, at the Church of the Ascension, for instance, on a Protestant's view of the humanity of the Catholic Church, or at Bellows's studio, or Henri's, where he spoke on the subject "Why there are Artists" to an audience of seventy-five, more or less. The faithful Fitzgerald and Gregg were usually present,—Gregg who had bought all of John Sloan's etchings while he often had a chip on his shoulder and wrote with the *Evening Sun's* vitriolic pen. Yeats and Sloan went for a week-end in Scarsdale when Yeats brought two parcels, one with a night-shirt, one with books and papers, including a play of Lady Gregory's that he read aloud; and once they went to Philadelphia, disheartening for Sloan although he recorded later that Yeats liked it. Sloan's mother, who had died in 1907, was buried in the church-yard of St. Thomas's Episcopal church in the suburb of Whitemarsh, which Marianna Sloan had decorated with two hundred life-size figures; but they stayed with

Sloan's father and sister and called upon Anshutz, Sloan's old teacher, the successor of Eakins. Anshutz, who was painting a portrait of himself, lectured in New York about that time, giving anatomical demonstrations to an audience that included Henri and Bellows, Sloan, Rockwell Kent and Walter Pach.

Years later Sloan often thought of Yeats walking along with his plunging gait, with his cane for a support, absorbed in conversation, now and then calling Sloan's attention to some incident in the street,—he described himself as "an old man in a hurry." One day they walked to Collier's to deliver a drawing that Sloan had made for *Collier's Weekly,* the office of which depressed Yeats, for it brought back the smell of Cassell's in London where he had submitted drawings with varying success. Once they walked to the Astor Library to spend an afternoon, Yeats reading Montalembert's *Monks of the West* while Sloan looked over *Burlington* magazines, interested in articles on Cézanne but still more interested in watching two scrub-women at work there. He painted these two scrub-women the following week. On another occasion Yeats insisted that he could cure Sloan's lame back by an all day's walk up-town and over the river, beginning on Riverside Drive where Sloan delighted in the colour of the Palisades in the morning light. It was red brown purple blue, he said, but Yeats would have none of this: he would not permit Sloan to linger, saying that the medicinal part of the walk was to have no dawdling, whether to admire, look or talk. They took the street-car to Van Cortlandt Park, went on to Yonkers, crossed on the ferry, and, climbing, walked on to the Hackensack valley, returning for Dolly's dinner in Twenty-third Street.

There was a time in 1911 when, for some weeks at least, Yeats worked along with Sloan in the studio garret, for his room at Petitpas' was small and he missed his Dublin studio, with which he could not bear to sever his connection. So for a while he sent certified cheques to pay the landlord for holding this, although it seemed a great waste of money. At Sloan's he was painting the self-portrait that John Quinn had commissioned, while Sloan worked on his own "Isadora Duncan Dancing," using a small easel while Yeats used the big one, Dolly interrupting the work to give them lunch. Not that one could interrupt Yeats, who was always ready to stop and talk, for which both Dolly and Sloan upbraided him; for concentrated work was difficult for him and he either failed to finish his work or he finished it too much and altogether. One day when a lady fortune-teller had prophesied to him that he was to have a "steady occupation" in the future, Sloan said she was evidently referring to the present portrait, for it dragged on week after week while Yeats idled and talked and for Sloan the picture became a bugaboo. At one point Henri was pleased with it,* but, in spite of Sloan's warning to "go easy and finish it," Yeats laboured away until he had beaten it to death, something he often did, spoiling many pictures that at a certain stage had been very good. In how many cases the picture slipped away because he never knew at what point to stop, while he

* In 1910 Sloan painted a sketch in oils of Yeats and Henri together in his studio.

had his ups and downs, in good spirits one day because of a happy dream he had had that night. "A happy dream lingers with me the whole day," he said. As for his failure with this self-portrait, Sloan reproached him cruelly, only to be sorry for it later, for "the thing was painted out and away," he noted in his diary, "and no scolding could bring it back." While Sloan was ashamed, Yeats, for the first time, was disheartened. But he went on working at the picture; he was still working three days later and he continued to work while the Sloans were moving, while their Lares and Penates, their books and the etching-press, along with the piano, were carted away. When two van-loads had gone Yeats said he had finished. The movers came back and took away his easel, along with the mirror from which he had worked.

How did the two regard each other? Sloan said that Yeats's pencil sketches were, as a rule, a "little sweet"; but he would have been ready to second, no doubt, Henri's praise of the portraits in Dublin, Yeats's best pictures which Sloan was never to see. For the rest, Sloan defended him fiercely against another artist who said Yeats was "an awful example of the artist's life,—old, poor, a failure, etc." Said Sloan in his diary, "The idiot! Mr. Yeats is a tremendous success. He has lived and had the poet's joy, still young in spirit, attracting young people around him." Meanwhile, he wrote in 1910 that Yeats gave him "very important helps in my thought about my work"; and thirty years afterwards he was to add, "Henri, in the formative period, and J. B. Yeats later, were the two great influences in my life." In what did Yeats's influence consist? How did he contribute to John Sloan's development and education? Partly by weaning him away from habits of mind that were detrimental and partly in more positive matters of feeling and thought.

In the first place, these were the years of Sloan's active socialistic phase when he was in the heat of radicalism, when he was given to questionable statements about the "socialism" of Jesus Christ and tried to convert stragglers on park benches. While Sloan never lost his socialist feeling, Yeats, as a younger man, had been interested in the socialist movement in England, for, sympathetic with William Morris and old Whitmanian that he had been, he was drawn to radical thinking as long as it was human. He enjoyed, as Sloan recorded, parts of Bakunin's *God and the State,* a copy of which Rockwell Kent had given to Sloan, and, hearing Eugene Debs speak, he said all Americans were preachers but that Debs was at least the highest example of the type. But he was concerned about the danger of an artist's meddling with propaganda, even if he kept this out of his work, and Sloan had become argumentative, for which Yeats rebuked him, saying that he was losing his good manners and his humour. Worse still, said Yeats, he was losing his feeling for truth. "It is not because I am faithless but because I dread the clash of tongues that I do not come to see you," he wrote on one occasion. "In the clash of tongues that modest maiden Truth disappears and her place is taken by the lady Falsehood, all bedizened and with cheeks highly rouged,—she is also very voluble and intimidating and so rapid in speech that you cannot get in a word, and that does not suit me at all, who like to do my own share of the talk." Again he wrote, "I love the give and take of quiet conversation—but I hate wrangling and the uproar and noise of newspaper polemics," and "When my family were all young I used to say to them, 'For God's sake don't form opinions. Let us have a quiet house' . . . That is why they have so much imagination and a well developed artistic sense. I notice artists and poets play with opinions but never come to any final conclusion—always do they seem aware that every opinion can be revised . . . I have always said we should hold our opinions loosely."

This was the burden of several letters that Yeats wrote to Sloan and that presently had their effect on this sensitive painter,—for another instance, "Poets and artists share with God Almighty the capacity for seeing both sides of any question. The prisoner is dear to them as the judge and the judge as the prisoner. Tolstoy teaches this again and again." And elsewhere, "Only minor artists and poets meddled with propaganda—except in their unripe youth. Dante and Hugo are not exceptions, for God Almighty took good care to have them both exiled, so that perforce they gave all their thoughts single-minded to poetry . . . If a man would be an artist, he must make his choice and abandon contention. Goethe and Shakespeare never touched the abhorred thing." With artists, Yeats was always saying, opinions and ideas must never be permitted to possess the mind, for "each opinion becomes in its turn a husk out of which has dropped all nourishment." He added, "Artists are wealthy noblemen who own many castles which they occupy from time to time but never permanently," and he appealed from Sloan drunk with argument to the sober Sloan whom he so loved, "There is no violence and no contention in those pictures I wrote about" (in one of the three articles he wrote on Sloan*). "They issued from a calm mind—calm is not the word—a mind in high tension at harmony with itself, fervent and delighted—like the sleep of a spinning top, as Carlyle calls it somewhere."

When the first world war began, Yeats remarked to Sloan, "Your pacifism is worse than the war, for it is far more polemical," and about this time he wrote also to me, "Sloan likes to be in a minority of one . . . and he generally succeeds in his wish. He is now a pacifist. I am waiting to see him separate from all the other pacifists and become his own particular pacifist. He should stick to his painting, but he won't." No, Sloan kept saying that no one could force him ever to wear a uniform, that he was proof against patriotism, the last refuge of the scoundrel, and that he would walk blocks to avoid any demonstration of a patriotic nature, the kind that Childe Hassam, for instance, loved to paint. Asked to contribute an etching to some series to celebrate the father of his country, he replied, "The subjects of the illustrations don't interest me. Many of them are to illustrate events that happened only in the fevered imagination of the fakers of patriotic history." Regarding brass hats in general as "inflated football players,"† he preferred to make cartoons for *War—What For?*—a question that could still be put in

* In *Harper's Weekly, The Seven Arts* and *The Freeman.*

† Sloan never lost his dislike and suspicion of military men and uniforms. In the year of his death, 1951, he mentions in his diary that, walking in New York, he was stopped by a parade: "We saw scores of military rolling stock, all shiny, all men's helmets new, looked like animated Christmas toys, silly, infantile, but *dreadful.*"

1914; and he asked, "Suppose we agree to call this country a province of England or France or Germany,—does it make any difference to me or any other working man?" To these emotional remarks Yeats replied that "pride of country" was "a great influence for good," explaining this view in terms that were very convincing,* pointing out at the same time why the Germans were so dangerous, like "the cruel inquisitors and persecutors of the Middle Ages." In these latter "the ecclesiastical logic had dried away," he wrote, "the vital flow of individual feeling, so that they were quite content to be merely parts of a machine," and the Germans were like these "mediæval bachelor priests 'bled white' by a long course of appalling education." He quoted John O'Leary's remark that even to save his country a man "should not weep in public and he should not lie," but that did not mean a country was not worth saving; and Yeats objected, moreover, to some of Sloan's cartoons, describing them as "violent and repulsive."

* "I think pride of country is a great influence for good. Why is the Hindu such a poor helpless creature? Because he is not permitted to have pride of country. The Japanese on the other hand is a man of self-respect and almost too proud, so Quinn tells me. The faults of the Irishman, his foolish swagger and wild exaggeration of himself and everything is because, notwithstanding his love for his native land, he is not allowed to have pride in it. It enrages him to remember that it is nothing to be an Irishman—people only laugh at his claims. The Scotch on the other hand have this pride, for though nominally without home rule they have it in reality—no English member of Parliament ever interferes with the Scotch members.

"The individual personality is enormously strengthened by the national personality—a Frenchman is more himself because of Paris." —Letter of J. B. Yeats to John Sloan.

In the end, Sloan was glad that Germany was defeated, because, he said, it meant the defeat of "efficiency."

To counteract these tendencies, Yeats appealed to Dolly, in whom they were even more active than they were in Sloan, "You are the wife of a man of heart and a man of genius with whom it is always a pleasure to associate (at least when he refrains from delivering knock down blows)"; and again, "Your husband is miraculously sensitive and light-hearted except when he forgets he is an artist and becomes a philistine squabbling with squabblers." As a result, in part, of this, Sloan spoke volumes when he wrote in his diary, "One must strive for good nature," and later, when he had recovered his full equilibrium, "I lost my sense of humour about the war a good deal of the time. J. B. Yeats scolded me." In this, without doubt, Yeats influenced Sloan as he influenced him in other ways, largely because he so greatly admired the artist, "finding fault yet breathing deference and compliment," he wrote, adding, "Your imagination is always dramatic." Elsewhere he remarked that Sloan's imagination was "Gothic," saying, "There is what Ruskin, speaking of northern art, called the 'mountain gloom' in everything you paint, and in your talk also. You have it in you to be one of the greatest artists." In qualification he observed, "You still have some way to travel (though I am not at all sure that you are not already arrived—on this question I often waver)." But he praised the "historian of New York" whose work had often a "poetic light" that reminded him of Giorgione. "One has to live many days with one of his pictures to find its sweetness, its poetic charm," said Yeats, who admired Sloan's severity too, the self-restraint of a man who would not be deceived although constantly looking for visions of tenderness and beauty. He asked why

Sloan's pictures of the ugly always attracted.* But he found the colour "barbarous" in a few of Sloan's experimental landscapes, and some of his work he did not like at all, believing it "done for effect . . . sometimes to shock or astonish people, which is the way of little artists." These pictures, he said, were "painted and drawn with a kind of violence and the colour deliberately unsympathetic." Yeats reproved Sloan also for a certain "carelessness," saying that an "ability to paint hands and feet" marked the artist and that in this respect Sloan fell short. "This is the age of athleticism and of pretty girls," he wrote. "Everyone is interested in the subtle beauties of well made ankles and everyone watches hands. Yet your hands and your ankles? Here truth is not *slurred,* it is despised as not worth while. If you had given as much study to hands and ankles as you have given to faces and to the torso, many a rock of offence and stone of stumbling would be removed from the pathway of your friends."

In this imputation of "carelessness" Yeats here echoed certain misgivings in Sloan's own mind; for, just as he too felt the danger of propaganda in his work, so he was beginning to question Henri's teaching. Asking himself, "Am I think-

* "It might be asked why do pictures of the ugly always attract, while from the ugly in life all except artists flee away? The fact is that men seek self-discipline with an interest just as strong as that which impels them to pleasure. I have walked among these streets with Mr. Sloan and have noticed with what a 'horrid' show of mysticism, awe and delight he would look at everything. 'Pain braces,' says Blake, 'and pleasure relaxes.' Mr. Sloan is of the kind who braces himself. Feeling, whether it be sorrow or hope or love, is avid of the truth, and poets and painters of feeling have an instinct for the truth which is part of their equipment."—J. B. Yeats, *The Seven Arts,* June, 1917.

YEATS AT
PETITPAS', 1910

TEA FOR ONE (HELEN), 1948

ing too much about art," he felt that Henri had not thought enough about it, that in his devotion to "life" and "animated statement," he had tended to slight deliberation, study and depth. Guy Pène du Bois told a story about a girl student he had known when he and she were both in Henri's classes and whom he encountered many years later working away at the Art Students' League, side by side with all the other beginners. Yet Henri had called her a "genius" and she had made quite a stir. Du Bois, who had come to teach at the League, asked her what she was doing there, and she answered, "Trying to learn to paint," as if Henri had never taught her anything, and Sloan was almost to feel this way when, after the Armory Show, he was to change his whole view of art and study. Here Yeats was already seconding his questionings and doubts; for, saying that "distinction is what Henri's splendid painting lacks," Yeats did not like the consequences of Henri's teaching. Nor did he regard Henri as an original thinker. Humble enough about himself, "a born portrait painter imprisoned in an imperfect technique," Yeats said, he was severe in his judgments and many of his remarks about Sloan and his friends rebuked Henri's "Don't think of art. Paint life." As he criticized Sloan's "carelessness," he said Luks had "everything except art" and that in his work there was "no thought and none of the labour of premeditation"; and, greatly liking Glackens, who painted, he felt, as a poet should,—for himself, and not for the crowd, like Zuloaga,—he found in Glackens also something missing. As a colourist, Yeats wrote to Sloan, he was "far ahead" of Renoir, but beside Renoir's his figures were "thin and papery." This was Renoir's "sole advantage over Glackens" but it was a great one; and the reason was that Renoir had "looked longer at Rubens."

Now Henri had been quite indifferent to "looking at Rubens," or any other old masters but Frans Hals and Velasquez,—and one or two others who suggested his own "animated statement,"—and only after the Armory Show did Sloan begin to look at them and largely as a result of the modern movement. Here again Yeats, the "most acute and prophetic critic of my work," as Sloan said later, contributed to his education, questioning the work of his master and his friends and charging him never to stop at a sketch but, as Turner would say, "carry the drawing further." * He was also continually telling Sloan that he "must not miss" this or that, the Degas at the American Art Galleries, the Monets at Knoedler's, the Sisleys or the Manets or the work of El Greco,—that "Hogarth of spiritual ecstasy," as Yeats put it. How vacuous beside these were many of the modern painters. "Go to Knoedler's and see the finished work of Orpen," for instance. "The technique is a candle by which you can see

* "Why does a painter or poet finish his work to the last degree, 'filling every rift with ore,' as Keats advised? I think it is to give it importance and force, to make it a veritable something."—Letter of J. B. Yeats to John Sloan.

Later, discussing the Independents show of 1917, Yeats wrote to Sloan, "I saw innumerable sketches but no pictures—beginnings but nothing accomplished—except your picture of the woman with her foot on the bed. I mean that there was no co-ordination, no attempt to organize and develop a unity . . . The whole might be compared to a tuning of the fiddles preliminary to a musical performance.

"The difference between a sketch and a picture is the difference between an inflammatory speech from a soap-box ignoramus who with the gift of speech is without knowledge, and the work of a serious and therefore exact thinker."

Sloan once wrote that by "lack of finish" Yeats meant "unrealized form."

that the cupboard is empty." Then there was Bakst on Fifty-seventh Street also,—"an engineer who has strayed in among the artists, his inspiration the cold energy of the engineer, delighting in engineering inventions of patterns, etc., to artists worthless." And how often had Sloan looked at the Rembrandts in the Metropolitan Museum?—"faces in deep obscurity and *all modelled to the last degree.* In all other artists including Whistler the modelling disappears when the face is in shadow,—no one but Rembrandt could model faces in shadow."

No doubt Yeats was thinking here of Sloan's own "mountain gloom," the "richly coloured darkness," for instance, of "McSorley's Back Room," which, as he wrote in *Harper's Weekly,* drew one's attention and held it,—one could "never be tired of peering in that gloom." Just so, one never tired of looking to the far horizon when night was coming on, and every painter, from the time of Leonardo, had felt the charm of chiaroscuro. To paint it, Yeats said, "is to make a picture of infinity,"—Sloan, he felt, was one of the few who had done so,—and in all his suggestions and criticisms the sympathctic Yeats kept in his mind the nature of the man he was addressing. For he greatly admired and loved both the painter and the man who had "the quiet artist's courage, the courage to be himself," which made his conversation so interesting also. Yeats saw in Sloan "the artist and poet, solitary, self-immersed in his own thoughts," with "no desire to impress other people," but with "the kind of spontaneity which makes his pictures refreshing to the eye wearied with conventional art." For the rest, human as Yeats was, he delighted in "this artist's message . . . that human nature has a perennial charm."

## CHAPTER IX

# GLOUCESTER: THE ARMORY SHOW

BEGINNING in 1914, Sloan spent five summers at Gloucester, with its fishing village atmosphere, on Cape Anne, where many artists gathered,—too many, Sloan felt in the end,—and where he and Dolly rented a small red cottage. Sally Stanton lived near by, a freckled pug-nosed little girl who followed him about like a puppy. He painted several pictures of her turning somersaults on the grass or sitting on the limb of an old apple-tree.

This move to Gloucester marked a new phase in Sloan's life, for thereafter almost all of his summers were spent out of the city and he virtually gave up painting the pictures of New York so many of which had been prompted by the summer life there. For summer was the open season and the artist's hunting ground when people came out and lived on the roofs and in the streets. But his conversion to socialism had made him self-conscious in choosing subjects that might be associated with propaganda, and the teaching that he also began in 1914 led him rather into figure work and landscape. "Teaching began to stir my interest in painting the figure," he said, "I wanted to keep a little ahead of my students"; and this was only one outward sign of a deep inner change which the Armory Show had induced the year before. For the Armory Show had revolutionized his thinking about art. As Sloan said later, "I began consciously to work from plastic motives more than from what might erroneously be called 'story-telling' motives." In short, summering at Gloucester, the Armory Show, teaching and social consciousness had weaned him away from painting "Sloans," the popular name for his early pictures, a name that he resented when he felt he had gone far beyond this work.

Some years later Sloan returned to the painting of New York scenes with more consciously formal motives and "orchestral colour," his phrase for the palette, greatly enlarged, that was already supplanting what he came to regard as his old timid browns and greys. Meanwhile, as his interest in the city waned, his interest rose in landscape, as well as in small-town-life scenes and pictures of the sea, and he began to work regularly out of doors every day, not waiting for a subject to arouse him. His city pictures had been painted from memory; he had seldom even drawn in the streets. At most he had made a slight sketch on a scrap of paper, coming home to paint his picture or to etch; although he had attempted out-door sketching at Flushing one afternoon, attracted by the copper beeches and the birches and oaks there. He had even tried landscape sketching in oil near Philadelphia, when he was visiting his mother, but the results had never satisfied him, while, working in Gloucester, in the open air, he found himself bringing his colour up "from the low tonality," as he put it, "of the early things." In one of his later notes he was to write, "Landscape is the very best way to wake up your colour sense," while teaching you to "exercise freedom in editing nature"; for, as he went on, in painting a head you hesitate to leave out an eye or a chin but you can omit with impunity a brook or a tree. He added, however, about landscape painting, that he stuck pretty faithfully to nature, sometimes leaving details out but rarely putting details in that did not exist in the scene he was painting. He continued with this interesting note on a younger painter: "I can remember that back in Gloucester when Stuart Davis was still very young and painting what you call representational pictures, he was already taking things from different parts of the landscape to put in his compositions. That was a sign that he was beginning to work abstractly." *

The landscapes that Sloan made in Gloucester in 1914 were his earliest response, he felt, to the Armory Show in the use of texture-colour and a more linear way of handling brush-work. He said you could see Van Gogh's influence in some of this work, and the heightening of his colour sense was to meet the wishes of J. B. Yeats who had greatly liked, —in its place,—Sloan's "mountain gloom." Yeats, however, had written to him, "Your skies are sinister and gloomy curtains . . . by no means the *divine things* they really are—divine as contrasted with the terrestrial, as are pretty women and children among sluts and rowdies. In your personal presence I dared not say these things"; and Yeats had begged Sloan to look at some Cazins and notice how bright and light in colour were the skies in contrast to his own heavy browns and opaque purples. "Your early admiration for Eakins is your misdoing," Yeats remarked in a letter that was pro-

* Sloan referred elsewhere to Stuart Davis, the son of his old friend Edward Davis, as "the best exponent of the modern movement that we have. He really works with his intelligence."

phetic of the work Sloan was to do;* while he rejoiced that Sloan had gone to the country and that he had taken up landscape painting. "My test of a landscape is this," he said, —"does the sky and the distance die away *into nothingness* . . . I have never wept over a landscape but I have wept over a painted landscape, such as Hobbema or Constable paints,—modest truthful landscapes where the note is not forced, and where there is no indecent display of technique, only intensity of feeling."

Along with landscape, Sloan had taken up lithography,† while he developed in drawing a wood-cut manner, trying to get an effect as of "free wood engraving" in some of his illus-

* "The Pre-Raphaelite movement was a reaction against those browns and heavy tints. The painters before Raphael all used light and joyous colours. Ruskin was the prophet and teacher who brought about the change. He always maintained that joyous and innocent minds favoured joyous colours, such as are in the work of the painter of San Marco, that dark and heavy colours were allied with guilty and criminal minds,–he was nothing if not moral. But it is a fact that if you paint dark skies, all the other objects in the picture must be dark also–that I think is obvious.

"Your early admiration for Eakins is your misdoing. He modelled a head well when the light falls on it–the dark side is always opaque, that is brown and dulled. Rembrandt's dark and shadowy faces are luminous through and through, showing modelling everywhere.

"Your dark and heavy colouring is alien to people's minds, and *stops the purchaser*. Don't be antagonistic; for these hints are of the highest importance, and don't drape all your streets and buildings in heavy browns."–J. B. Yeats to John Sloan.

† "The beauty of lithography is in those rare tender tones that you get only by drawing on the stone itself. A drawing that is made on paper and transferred to stone is not properly a lithograph, it has none of the qualities of a fine print. The stone has a finer surface than the finest paper in the world. It is like some wonderful crisp silk."–*Gist of Art*.

As for wood-engraving, Sloan admired the work of J. J. Lankes.

trations for magazines and books. He bought two books on Thomas Bewick, whom Audubon had visited in England, remarking, "Those old vignettes are beautiful things, full of humour and 'great' art . . . His tiniest prints are noble and spacious in design." Somewhat in Bewick's manner, he made a bookplate for Rockwell Kent, who had been staying on Monhegan island, finding his city resolutions melting away in this fisherman's world where men lived and toiled in a tremendous fashion. Kent liked a dinner of lentils, potatoes, onions, rice and lima beans "all stewed up together in their own blood" there, while Henri, who was at Monhegan too, "went into raptures," Kent said, over this Bewick-esque bookplate that Sloan had made. But, while there was no cooling of their old affection, Sloan and Henri were drawing apart, largely because of the Armory Show that marked a new epoch in American painting and put Henri's nose out of joint. Sloan had always fiercely defended Henri, his "art father," against the attacks and slurs of young and old, against Luks's "scrofulously offensive" remarks and Yeats's observation that Henri's work was "getting too empty." He was always saying that Henri's critics were unable to see the whole of his work, that his landscapes and city pictures were too little known and that people only knew his portraits, although Henri himself had been to blame for this, for he chose to appear solely as a portrait painter. While his landscapes were among the finest things he did, he made a point of keeping them out of sight, for he saw that the critics were confused when they could not pigeonhole a man. But, grateful as Sloan continued to be for Henri's revolt against artifice and the reign of French nineteenth-century academic art, he cared less and less himself for Henri's "flourishing brush-work" and his precepts about rapidity and "spontaneous statement." Always looking up to him, Sloan had never dreamed of crossing him, but he found himself after the Armory Show going to school, a beginner, again, as if all of Henri's teaching had come to naught.

Henri, in short, had been dethroned, and not in Sloan's eyes only, for he was no longer the leader in American art,—this domineering older man who liked to lay down the law although he defended, abstractly, freedom of opinion. He bitterly resented the Armory Show, feeling that now he was out of things,—the things that he had been running so long himself,—and, while hurting his pride, it kept him, Sloan thought, from learning a great deal that might have been beneficial for his own work. But, living through the whole modern movement, Henri had not reacted to it. Blind or hostile to Renoir, Matisse and Picasso, he had cared only for Rouault, with a handful of Cézannes; nor, in all his years abroad, had he been interested in the great old masters to whom the ultra-moderns had opened Sloan's eyes. He had never mentioned Mantegna, Carpaccio, Bellini, and he had retained Eakins's love of the sombre and the heavy when Sloan himself was fighting for more colour. Sloan, who was thinking more and more about formal relationships in his work and what he called "the concept of the thing as it is known in the mind," had ceased to be interested in Henri's "surface painting," and he shocked his old mentor by insisting that solidity was the thing to strive for, not "brush-work," however graphic, however dynamic. He no longer cared to see how a picture was painted, for he realized that most of the great masterpieces were really inscrutable, graphic as they might be.

John Sloan was not the only painter who had grown away from Henri. Nor was he the only artist of the middle generation whose work was revolutionized by the Armory Show, although George Luks was indifferent to it or hostile to the futurists and cubists to whom he referred in words that curdled the blood. Or so James Huneker said in an article about him. Arthur B. Davies made desperate efforts to adjust himself to the new men, and, failing, lost confidence in himself and disappeared for a time, after which his fragile figures, which had lacked much of the sap of life, began to show a cubist influence. Boardman Robinson presently remodelled his whole career and began searching and experimenting, like Sloan himself. Giving up cartooning, becoming a painter, he studied composition and design and made analytical studies of the old masters in preparation for the later murals that Sloan was to admire so much as the best that had ever been done in the country. Sloan's only qualification was that they were not to be compared with the work of the great Mexican painters Rivera and Orozco. Paradoxically enough, the Armory Show, which had dethroned Henri, had for the first time brought Eakins to the front, for from that moment the old Philadelphia painter was accepted as one of the great figures of American art. Dying in 1916, "the Philadelphian whom Philadelphians never thought it worth while to honour,"—as a critic remarked the following year, at the time of the Eakins exhibition in New York,—triumphed at last with the disciples who had come in as the "Eight" and who had been largely responsible for the Armory Show. In this "grand provincial," as Walter Pach called him, many of the new painters saw a precursor.

For the organizers of the great exhibition of "Ellis Island art," that show of "asafoetida," as one critic called it, were a group of twenty-five, an extension of the "Eight," who had shown in 1910 the "Independent Artists." * As an emblem of the Armory Show they had chosen the Pine Tree, connecting the American Revolution with this event in the world of art that was also a declaration of independence. The artists in question were aware that something was happening in European art of which they wanted first-hand knowledge, for in general Americans had been unaware of anything of the kind since 1885 when Durand Ruel brought over and showed the first Impressionists in New York. It was true that Alfred Stieglitz had been showing the new artists since 1908, but he reached a very small audience at "291," † almost as small as John Quinn reached with his

* "The best exhibition ever held on this continent," John Sloan called the first Independent show, which opened on April 1st, 1910, when three large floors were crowded to the point of suffocation. The throng packed the sidewalks outside trying to get in. "A small squad of police came on the run," Sloan noted in his diary, adding, "Wonderful to think that an art show could be so jammed. At least 2000 people the first evening." This was entirely a show of American art.

† Sloan readily admitted that Stieglitz should be credited for first showing the Post-Impressionists, but he did not personally cotton to Stieglitz, who felt, Sloan said, that he "owned ultra-modern art" and resented the rivalry of the "Eight" and the Armory Show. He had been very angry about the "Independents" exhibition, feeling it had stolen his thunder. "I went to 291 once," Sloan said in a speech at the Art Students' League, "and he talked off one ear. It has grown

private collection of a handful of them before Quinn helped to finance the Armory Show. This exhibition was not only a revolt against decadent academic art but a revolt in favour of a native art also,—which led to the discovery of Eakins,—revealing in chronological sequence the starting-points and influences out of which the Post-Impressionists had grown. Beginning with Ingres and Delacroix, the classic and romantic antipoles, it traced an unbroken historical line through Courbet to the painters who embodied the complex feeling of the life of the day. Arthur B. Davies, whose work had been selling well, helped to back the show with his own money, and, going to Paris with Walt Kuhn, he had fallen in with Walter Pach, who had been living there virtually for the last ten years. Pach introduced the others to the painters and sculptors whose work they all presently chose for the Armory Show.

Years later John Sloan said that Walter Pach was really the man who had made the Armory Show memorable for its quality and richness, and he was indignant that Pach's enthusiasm and scholarship were ignored by those who had told the story of the exhibition. For Pach was the only one who had known the new French artists and was able to select their work and plan the show. Sloan himself, who was busy with the *Masses,* had helped to hang the pictures, while he found "something poetic" in the committee meetings, but he never wavered in his belief that Pach was the "real genius" behind it all whose judgment had given the show its great importance. Pach had known the new sculp-

---

back pretty well, but I never returned to 291 . . . I tried to keep away from him, out of his hair."

tors as well as the painters, and, as Maurice Prendergast was the first American to feel the quality of Cézanne, so Pach had been one of the first to write about him. He had written about Renoir and Monet, with both of whom he had frequently talked, and Matisse, whom he had first met in the villa of the Steins at Fiesole, had etched a portrait of this American critic and painter. In Paris, Pach had met two men who had actually known Delacroix, the artist whose *Journal* he was to translate,—as he wrote the first book on Ingres in America or England,—and he had fallen in with Redon, Rouault, Brancusi and Derain, one or two of whom had become his friends. He had talked often with Picasso and Braque in the rue de Fleurus at Gertrude Stein's, and with Jacques Villon he had written and published a commemorative study of Duchamp-Villon, the brother of Marcel Duchamp who lived in New York. When someone enquired where was the "nude" in Duchamp's picture, the "Nude Descending the Stairs" in the Armory Show, it was Pach who asked where was the moon in the Moonlight Sonata. The translator of Elie Faure's *History of Art,* Pach had met Thomas Eakins too and written one of the first appreciative essays on him, and he had often visited Albert P. Ryder in his back room in the tenement-house in New York. He had ploughed through the debris amid which "Uncle Ryder," the friend of all the slum children and his poor fellow-lodgers, had "realized his golden dream" in works of art, while comfort and discomfort, fair weather and foul, seemed all the same to him, as Pach was to observe in *Queer Thing, Painting.* Ryder, the child of New Bedford and the painter of "Jonah and the Whale," who might have painted the Spouter Inn and Queequeg, had lived in New York almost as obscurely as Melville.

For Pach the pre-war years in Paris were a time of great expansion when he felt what he called "big things ahead," and he also felt that Americans had been living "off the canned foods of art" when there was fresh meat and fresh fruit on these French tables. "The reason for an interest in modern art is very simple," he observed, "that it is the only kind we can produce," while he had himself a historical perspective not only of European and Asiatic art but of the art of the Incas, Aztecs and Mayans. Agreeing with Renoir that the museum is "the real teacher of all the great men" and what he called "the mariner's compass of art," he felt that to falsify its indications was to throw artists out of their course, perhaps on the rocks. Because of this he wrote *Ananias or the False Artist* to specify the modern counterfeits of art and show how important it was to exercise judgment regarding the choice of objects for museums. Attacking the simulacra of art, the mere "coloured photographs" that had such a powerful influence on the taste of the time, exposing the artists who, he felt, betrayed their noble calling, he made enemies right and left in the most powerful circles. But this modernist who knew the ancient arts better than most of the academicians, as he knew by heart the great museums of the world, and as he knew the American public from travelling and lecturing through the South and the West, was no less humble than he was courageous. "One is never too far advanced in art to renounce humility," he wrote, "as a primary need in one's attitude toward the subject." He regarded the masters with an all but religious veneration.

Now Cézanne's work had shown Pach the greatness of Signorelli, whom he said he had never "truly seen,"—although he had spent weeks copying a Signorelli painting,—and just so it was the ultra-moderns who opened John Sloan's eyes to what he called "the real mystery of the old masters." He meant their "thought processes" and the "technique which gives power to form," and it was after the Armory Show that he began to study them, sharing for the first time Pach's feeling about museums. "Brush-work" and what he called "drawing with paint, leaving the brush-technique on the surface" came to seem to him mere "paint slinging," and, although he was never to paint abstractly, he absorbed just the same a great deal from the new abstract French artists. He was excited by their concern with structure and particularly texture, while he owed to some of the modern men what he described as a "new freedom in using colour graphics." He saw for the first time at the Armory Show paintings by Renoir and Van Gogh, both of whom influenced him in very large measure when he was trying to enlarge the scope of his palette. At the same moment, the primitive Italians and Flemings largely took for him the place that Frans Hals had taken in his earlier interest, for, with his liking for the kind of work that showed how it was done, he had only admired these old masters distantly and slightly. He remembered how, looking at reproductions, he had passed by anything with a religious motif, feeling that "that wasn't life" and that the painting was "tight" as compared with the work of the "fluid brush boys." But now he began to see in Giotto or Carpaccio what the modern movement was driving at,* for Picasso and Matisse had taught him to appreciate plastic form and textural significance and what he called "the sign-making graphics of painting." He had had no use himself for "realism without realization," but Cézanne spoke volumes to Sloan when he said, "Nature's forms are not art's forms" and "I have not tried to reproduce nature, I have represented her." For Sloan, in a word, the Armory Show was an education and also "the beginning of a journey into the living past. The blinders fell from my eyes," he said, "and I could look at religious pictures without seeing their subjects. I was freed to enjoy the sculptures of Africa and prehistoric Mexico because visual verisimilitude was no longer important. I realized that these things were made in response to life, distorted to emphasize ideas about life, emotional qualities of life." So John Sloan was to write thirty-five years later.

What Walter Pach said about the Fauves, that they had inaugurated "a period of *conscious purpose*" as compared with "the reliance on instinct of the time before," †—all this, generally true of artists, was true specifically of Sloan, who

* "The academic painters of the nineties paid lip service to the old masters, but if Giotto had been reborn in the last century he would have been refused exhibition space. If there were a rebirth today of a man with the same brain, glands, personality as Giotto or Carpaccio, he would have a chance for recognition, thanks to Picasso, Cézanne, Matisse, Rouault, Redon—none of whose work resembles Giotto or Carpaccio in any degree. The ultra-moderns have prepared the way for artists who will come along to paint life with formal consciousness."—John Sloan, Talk at the Hudson Guild, 1949.

† Walter Pach, *The Masters of Modern Art.*

was ready, at forty-two, for this new dispensation. Aroused to a sense of plastic values, and feeling almost for the first time that "the making of a picture could be a joyful thing," he understood what George Moore meant when he spoke of the failure of the nineteenth century in making painting a handmaiden to literature. The Armory Show revealed to Sloan "how far the mind's sight differs from eyesight," and he felt that these artists had freed the world from "servitude to merely optical effects," returning it to the "fundamental root principles of art." Sloan could not say too often that our eyes have been sharpened by photography and our brains dulled by the same process, while the medicine of ultra-modern art had almost brought about a cure for the disease of "eyesight imitation." But was this art really new? There was nothing new in art. "What has happened is just a return to the old standards: some of them African, some Aztec, some Hindu, some Negro, some Chinese, some European. A return to those old arts has been dubbed the 'modern movement.' " *

Thus the Armory Show, that turning-point in American art-history, was also a turning-point in the life of Sloan, for it opened a new epoch in his work and outlook. He often said later that the artists of America were producing amazing fruits from the seeds that were sown at that great exhibition, even though he might have agreed with Maurice Prendergast that there was "too much Oh-my-God! art" in it.

* One of Sloan's notes, 1947.

## CHAPTER X

# SLOAN AND HIS PUPILS

SLOAN, WHO AS A YOUNG MAN had questioned the value of art-schools, or felt at least that they were not good for him,—although he had studied himself for a while with Anshutz,—found himself only a few years later teaching in Henri's New York school and doing his best to make up for the master's absence. Indeed, from that moment for the rest of his life Sloan remained a teacher, whether of private pupils or at various art schools, and he became a famous teacher, severely conscientious, with what he called a "sharp but honest tongue." It was not as sharp as Anshutz's tongue, —"like a razor dipped in sulphuric acid," as someone remarked who knew the old man well; and Sloan himself said that he was harsh because the students frightened him, highly strung as he was, reserved and shy. Histrionic also, his bellicosity was self-protective, like the clowning in which he said he indulged at parties—"taking the stage" to cover up his shyness,*—and his pupils were generally aware of the warmth of heart that accompanied his occasional attacks on them.

* Sloan remarked in one of his notes, "I am a human sandwich, a slice of modesty, a slice of reticence, sparsely buttered with wisdom, and a thick slice of ham (actor)."

Teaching for a living, Sloan also taught for the stimulus of it, for it "lashed him into a state of consciousness," and he found himself trying to prove in his work some of the things, he said, that he dug out of his sub-conscious to pass on to others. He had really begun to study, he added, when he began to teach, and teaching obliged him to clarify his own motives in painting. He called it "scraping the attic of the brain," finding there the principles that one could not "lay" after one unearthed them, and, having started to harp in his teaching on certain technical ideas, he said, these continued to pursue him for the rest of his life. Thus teaching played a vital part in his own work as an artist while keeping him at the same time young and humble, for what could be better for an artist than contact with hungry minds, as long as he was not forcing his theories on them? Teaching, meanwhile, with illustrating, made it possible for Sloan to carry on his proper and personal work, for he depended until 1911 on the word-charade puzzles for the Sunday *Press* that remained his only regular source of income. He did these weekly drawings for twelve years.

Beginning at the Henri school, Sloan taught here and there before he took up his work at the Art Students' League, with which he was to be connected for twenty-two years,—for instance, at the Pittsburgh Art Students' League, for one day a week, travelling back and forth on over-night trains. Henri procured this position for him, as he turned over to Sloan the offer of an art-school directorship at Columbus, Ohio, but Sloan was unwilling to leave New York while Pittsburgh interested him, for the mills gave great character to the atmosphere. It was splendid, he said, to look down in the evening across the Monongahela when the red sun was setting over the hills and mountains to the west. Sloan had numbers of private pupils,—he gave Vernon Howe Bailey* instruction in etching, as he gave points to George Bellows and Rockwell Kent; and he shared briefly a school with the sculptor Archipenko, as he took over George Luks's school in 1934. Luks was found dead one night under the Sixth Avenue elevated railway, and a group of students who had loved him stayed on with Sloan while various new pupils came to join them. Luks's old studio was a ramshackle romantic place, a fire-trap with uncertain heating but superb light, at the rear of the American Art Galleries on Twenty-third Street, and Sloan, who had sometimes found Luks obnoxious, regarded a few of his pictures, at least,—"The Wrestlers," for one,—as "very great works of art." At this time Sloan regretted the League, from which he had resigned, although he was to return to it a few years later. Devoted to teaching as he was, he conducted summer art-classes at Gloucester, where he said the docks were littered with Charles Hawthorne's pupils. He shared the class one summer with Randall Davey, Henri's pupil, and A. F. Levinson was one of his own pupils there.†

* Sloan had known Bailey in Philadelphia in 1894 when they were both members of the Charcoal Club, and he admired Bailey's drawings and water-colours of country scenes and streets in Italy and Spain. He marvelled over Bailey's life of adventure and work, for Sloan was always momentarily impressed by travelled "adventurous" people who made his own life seem "uneventful."

† Sloan greatly admired Levinson's "direct and sensitive" drawing. "Every stroke of his brush had graphic power," he said. "There are none of the American moderns who have his freedom from routine in composition or colour plan."

It was at the Art Students' League that Sloan became known as a teacher, beginning in 1916 and going on until 1938 with a break of five years in the early thirties. As late as 1910 Sloan had felt only contempt for the League, with which he had refused to have any connection, even declining to make a sketch for the "Fakir Show" catalogue there, for he said it was too academic an institution. Had he come to feel that any school is what the teachers make it? He was finally convinced that the League was the best art school in the country because it presented the widest range for students, from the ultra-conservative to the ultra-modern, and he was to be happy there for many years, while adding to the joy of several distinguished pupils. He was certainly not a proselytizer. He never attempted to make converts to art, for he felt that too many young people were trying to paint pictures who would have been better employed as designers or craftsmen, and he constantly told his pupils that they would never learn anything from him which would enable them to make any money. He followed Henri in often remarking, "Contemporary success means failure" and "There's nothing so ruinous for an artist as an easy success," the financial success that is doubly corrupting if the artist secretly yearns for the sort of things that money can buy. For then "he gets the taste of fine living, and that is the end of his independence." Sloan said, "If you want to be a painter, keep away from commercial art," and he would have agreed with Ingres not only that "drawing is the probity of art" * but that art is a kind of apostleship as well as a profession.

* "Painting is drawing, with the additional means of colour. Painting without drawing is just 'colouriness,' colour excitement."—John Sloan, *Gist of Art*.

In his method and style as a teacher, Sloan resembled Henri in some respects, as one can see by comparing his *Gist of Art* with Henri's earlier book called *The Art Spirit,* —largely compiled, like Sloan's, from his sayings in the class-room,—while he had been influenced also by William Morris Hunt's *Talks on Art,* a favourite of Henri's that Sloan read more than once. When he took up teaching at the League, he read Hunt again. But while Henri's instruction had been highly suggestive, and especially moving emotionally, Sloan felt its effects were far too evanescent, for it lacked the technical information that he himself set out to convey with his own abundant knowledge and rare gift of expression. Always honest, always helpful and almost always witty, he brought students to book when they were not "serious about playing," * when a young thing in the

"When you can make some drawings that will set a pattern for the rest of your life, then paint. Then it will be time enough to paint. Draw until you don't care if you never paint, then paint. Then you will have some things to paint that will take a lifetime to work out."—Unpublished talks to students.

"Sloan was an inspiring teacher. Painting, he said, was drawing with oil colour. *Drawing* was all important. 'Draw,' he said, 'draw everything you *see* or *imagine* or *dream of,* and draw in every conceivable way.' And so we students drew. Wherever we went, we were armed with sketch books. At night, in our own rooms, we turned out the lights and drew strange things without being able to see our papers. We drew from memory. We pretended we were Matisse and drew like him. Like Renoir, and drew like him. Like Picasso . . . always . . . with an effort to fathom the artist's thought processes, never with the idea of acquiring style cheaply."—Aaron Bohrod, in *College Art Journal,* 1950.

* "We're here to play . . . to play because we are serious about it . . . If you don't want to be serious about playing, do something of no account. Go into banking; buy collar buttons at five cents a dozen and sell them for five cents apiece."—*Gist of Art.*

class, for instance, was very coy with Sloan and he let her go on kidding him night after night. Appearing to like it, he said at last that she was such a cute little kitten he was afraid she would make a tough old cat. He sometimes appeared with a book in his hand or prints of Daumier lithographs, to show Daumier's wonderful way of picturing a crowd, or he would refer to El Greco's "eagerness" or observe that every square inch of an El Greco canvas was alive and moving. He said once, "That model should make you all feel like painting masterpieces," but he scarcely ever posed the model, for he was content, as he put it, with what "happened." Sometimes he made the students draw with their backs to the model, and in criticizing he raised his voice so that all the students might hear his comments on each painting. He had found that students took more seriously criticism of their work when it was actually addressed to the work of another, as mothers in clinics would only accept criticisms of their own child when the remarks were aimed at another's baby.

In retrospect, Sloan's pupils dwelt on the enthusiasm he aroused, his actual passion for expression, which started their "roots" growing, the "high things" he stood for, his generosity, and how he had "always been for the youth of today and a freedom that has both eyes open." They perceived behind the sharp tongue his goodness and sincerity and his deep faith alike in humanity and in art, while, usually acute, though not easily genial, he inspired his pupils to take notes on his talk, so that a fairly large body of his sayings survived him. "Consistency is the quality of a stagnant mind," he said once,—adding that he hoped his mind was sufficiently alive to outgrow tomorrow his ideas of today,—and he continued, "So don't take down what I say, like a court stenographer, for I shall soon say the opposite and both statements will be right." Again he remarked that people who took things too literally were not likely to get very much from him, and a reader of the notes saw at once that his most flexible and imaginative pupils were those who heard him say the most interesting things. One could have guessed their own quality from the quality of their notes, a few of which may be assembled, more or less at random:

The artist must have a calm excitement in life.

An artist should have a heart of fire and a brain of ice.

It is the job of the artist to correct what he sees by what he knows.

Artists are the only people in the world who really live. The others have to hope for heaven. That is why heaven is such a success as an idea.

There are no superiors among masters.

Be able to do a thing slowly and still keep it so that it has the look of impulse.

Of necessity, the artist cannot mingle with people as often as he would like but reaches them through his work.

Study the old masters' paintings—study them for ten years.

The poison of art started about 1860 when the camera came into use.

Through the influence of the camera, few artists know today the difference between the aspect and the concept of a thing.

Every generation is *the* generation to an artist.

Cubism is a sort of purgative that has cured art of the sickness of surface imitation.

You don't really see pictures in nature unless you are making them.

Facility is a dangerous thing. When there is too much technical ease the brain stops criticizing. Don't let the hand fall into a smart way of putting the mind to sleep.

Great art lies somewhere between naive and intellectual art.

A pencil or pen line on a piece of white paper hasn't the capacity of doing evil that a paint brush has.

Eyesight painting? It is terrible. Mind-sight—that is the secret.

Draw or paint as though you were running your hands over the model. Record tactile sensations.

If you were painting a ghost at midnight in a dense fog, they nevertheless would all have to be real in the painting.

A number of Sloan's pupils became well-known figures in the world of art, although not in every case as painters,—Angna Enters, the dancer, for one, and the Japanese photographer Sunami, who was later connected with the Museum of Modern Art. Others were Nat Smolin, who sculptured a head of Sloan, Joseph Pollet, the Swiss painter whom for a while Sloan considered the hope of American art,—at a time when Pollet's work was akin to Van Gogh's,—Otto Soglow, the black-and-white artist, Peggy Bacon, Reginald Marsh and Stirling Calder's son, Alexander Calder. Sloan told another, a woman painter whom he regarded as too clever by half, to draw with her left hand to overcome the poisonous facility that her right hand showed,—whereupon she "wept with fury," Sloan recorded; and there was another whose left hand was as facile as his right and similarly refused to take directions from the mind. What could Sloan say to rebuke this tendency to slickness? "There is only one thing left for you to do," he said, "pull off one of your socks and try with your feet." Some of these pupils made permanent records of the Sloan class,—for instance, Peggy Bacon in a dry-point, which led to a misunderstanding between teacher and pupil,*—and Otto Soglow, who made an etching of "Criticism Night" at Sloan's and a large lithograph entitled "Johnny's Place." (For, while few of his friends called him "John," and even Dolly called him "Sloan," some of his pupils referred to him as "Johnny.") In the latter, the master, in shirt-sleeves, with cigar in mouth and derby on head, stood behind a bar passing out schooners of beer, while various recognizable characters appeared sitting or dancing. "O. Soglow," who worked in a toy-factory painting baby rattles, spent much of his spare time illustrating the *Sloanian Nut,* the comic organ of the class that was printed on a large zinc plate furnished by a student who worked as a lithograph artist. One of the students described O. Soglow as the court jester of the class and said it was obvious that he had conceived there the idea of the "Little King" of the comic cartoons.

Sloan remembered Alexander Calder, the son of his old

* According to Sloan, Peggy Bacon told him twenty-five years later that she had been too shy to explain to him a misunderstanding in connection with her dry-point of the night class. "I had remarked that there was only one pretty face in the group, the author's, and that it must be a rather mean spirited person who would caricature everyone else. I had not studied the drawing closely enough to realize that her characteristic features had been acidly stated elsewhere in the composition, and she later told me that the pretty girl was Katherine Schmidt. All those years she was too scared to explain until we reminisced over a couple of highballs."—One of Sloan's "student notes."

sculptor friend, as studying in his own independent way, appearing with an enormous piece of architect's draughting-paper and setting this up at the rear of the class-room. He produced "great imaginative line drawings in charcoal that filled the whole space," Sloan said, and that were "very remarkable in quality from the first"; and it was at the Independents show that he exhibited his first wire sculpture, the subject being Romulus and Remus with the mother wolf. "This was all drawn," said Sloan, "with ingenious manipulation of a continuous thread of wire"; for Calder was "interested in the travels of the line, activating it, later abstracting it . . . twenty years before Picasso was photographed drawing with light." Walter Pach had written from Paris that "Sandy" was already well spoken of by some of the good artists he knew there in 1932, and Sloan was deeply interested in this "line drawing in space" in the work of Calder and Henry Moore as well. He said to Pach, "The only really abstract art-element is line. Light and shade, perspective, solidity and the rest all exist in nature. Line is the creation of the artist." *

* "The beginning of graphic art was the invention of the line; the most purely inventive portion of technique is the use of the line . . . You see something going along, a tree trunk—the gesture to show the line, you make it with your hand without thinking that you are drawing. Some very good sculpture is line drawing in space. Henry Moore and Alexander Calder eliminate bulk, tonality and draw with wire and cut-out form.

"Henry Moore's work has the essential beauty of line in three-dimensional space . . . He analyzes three-dimensional drawing down to the elemental thing which is important—the line.

"Moore's primary consideration is the line in space. He selects those movements which interest him, a hip, shoulder, arm, etc., and uses only as much form as is necessary to tie the selected linear

Of another pupil, Angna Enters, Sloan had been scarcely aware until he met her afterwards in the theatre when he found himself an "astonished, charmed and enthralled beholder of your dance creations," as he wrote in a letter of 1926. Coming from Milwaukee, she had entered his night-class hoping to study commercial art, and, as she put it, Sloan drove her out of art, for he saw no talent in her work. Only once in the less than two months that she came intermittently did Sloan even stop to examine her work, when he criticized her for working in line rather than mass, while she looked despondently at what to her were the hazy forms made by a Japanese student,—no doubt Sunami,—that obviously interested Sloan. This was her only contact with the teacher. But something that Sloan said caused her to change her direction, for it led her to realize that she should express through motion, in space, all the interest she felt in colour and form. What Sloan said was, "Remember, if there was no light in this room, the figure still would have the same form. The patches of light and shade you see are merely the accident of the way the light is placed." The remark was a revelation to Angna Enters, who said she was "struggling for something, she knew not what," and for the first time she was conscious of a sense of form, "not only in drawing, but in any expression." *

---

elements together—eliminating all other factual material."—Sloan, Unpublished notes.

* Angna Enters, *Silly Girl*. In this autobiography Miss Enters remembers saying to herself, "It's true, Sloan doesn't see anything in my work either. But what difference does it make whether I have talent or what anyone else thinks about it? What is important is that it gives me pleasure and I must do it as well as I can . . . From

Later, at one of her evening performances, Sloan was present with some of his friends, sitting in a box at the left of the stage, all of whom, Henri and Bellows among them, came to her dressing-room where Sloan stood shyly behind the others. But Angna Enters, seeing him, exclaimed, "Mr. Sloan, I must tell you I was in your class at the League and it was there I first had the idea of making theatre compositions." Sloan stammered, "Oh—were you? When was that?" and Henri protested, as Bellows grinned, "Why don't you say you were in *my* class? See, he doesn't even remember you." The following year she was struck by a remark of Henri, who came to tea with Sloan, "Don't ever become an expatriate. So many artists go abroad and never come back, and something happens to their work. You must never let that happen to you." In the meantime, Sloan had been carried away by her "compositions in dance form" that included "Moyen Age," "Viennese Waltz," the "Cat Dance," "Contredanse" and so on,—among them "Odalisque," interpreting the painting by Ingres,—finding her transformations amazing, the ways in which she changed her face, looking like a man, for example, or even a horse. Her psychopathic numbers also impressed him, and one pantomime in which the stage was black with only a white face dancing suggested Sloan's revelatory statement at the League. He sketched her again and again in the theatre, and he made two paintings of her, with a number of etchings; and she sent him from the Basque country a neck-scarf, a really beautiful thing, rich in tone, yellow, red and black.

---

such small moments do we shape our lives. And from that moment no one could deflect her from what she must do."

Another of Sloan's pupils, Don Freeman, who had come from California, admiring especially Sloan's illustrations and etchings, observed that the very appearance of the man, his jutting chin and sharp eyes, with his sheaf of steel-grey hair, "sang out his greatness." Working himself during the day as a trumpeter in a dance-band, Freeman said that Sloan's words were "sparks" that charged him "with a live current of inspiration" and that he had never seen or heard anything to beat Sloan, with his devastating wit and forceful flow of wisdom. "His generosity of spirit," said Freeman, "kept the class fastened to his invigorating words," as he praised the work of students that gave evidence of striving, and "something happened to me," he added, for "everywhere I went after that I saw colour problems. The city suddenly took on the aspect of one huge canvas, and whenever I saw something especially beautiful I would almost smell oil paint and turpentine." *

Many years later, an Italian pupil, Easoni Martino, wrote out his reminiscences of "Johnny" and the class, long after he himself had gone back to Italy where he owned a chestnut grove at Parma. At harvest time the chestnuts were big and most of them out of the burrs, but, even so, gathering them was like sticking youı hand in a porcupine's back when you had cleared the woods of underbrush and ferns. After a few weeks, he wrote, your hands were so sore that you scarcely dared to meddle for a month with pigment, and in fact Martino had become a Sunday painter; but he almost outdid Vasari in his warm-hearted gossip about the teacher he had revered in the early twenties. He noted that

* Don Freeman, *Come One, Come All.*

when he first studied with Sloan in 1919, the teacher's list of old masters was rather restricted, Rembrandt for the Dutch school and Goya and El Greco for the Spaniards, with Daumier and Gavarni, Hogarth and Leech. Luca Signorelli was the only Italian whom Sloan ever mentioned, and Martino could see analogies in Sloan's later paintings with those of the great stoic of Orvieto; but he saw in *Gist of Art* that Sloan had acquired a profound acquaintance with many old masters of all countries.

It pleased Martino to see that Sloan defied the desire of so many moderns to make room for their "abortions" by burning all ancient art, and he recalled some of Sloan's remarks and his great kindness in helping him when he undertook to work as an illustrator. Sloan sent him a set of sketches he had made explaining various ways of shading in order to get colour into his drawings. Then Sloan said one day, apropos of his belief that "What you know" matters, not "What you see,"—"When painting a landscape it is desirable to walk through the clumps and around the bushes, around the trees, the houses and the rocks. Familiarizing yourself in this way with the subject, you will get a better concept of the thing and not a visual and false snapshot." Again he said, "Painting is better than etching. If the work goes wrong you have only to scrape it off and start over again. In etching, if the work goes wrong you have to spend bitter days scraping, filing and hammering like a tin-smith and even then not get the thing right." Again, "Most art students are generous till it comes to squeezing their colour on the palette. Put as much colour on your palette as you think you'll need and a little over. Don't be stingy with your paint, it isn't worth it. Many pictures haven't become works of art simply because the artist tried to save a nickel's worth of colour." But Sloan could give lessons in economy also. Using one day as a pointer an old brush with hardened colour on it, Sloan, while giving his criticisms, combed this with his fingers, and, rubbing it for almost an hour, he was able to say to its owner at last, "You see, I have given you a new brush."

Once a week the master criticized the work which the students had done out of school, on Sundays or in their spare time during the week, and for those who lacked imagination he would suggest themes, the barber-shop, or the Elevated, or the Automat. One could always tell his mood from the colour of his necktie. If he came into class with a violet tie, the students all knew that he was depressed, and this was a warning to the initiated that they should be quiet or expect a "bawling out" in public. On the other hand, if he came in with a yellow-orange tie, they knew that somehow fortune had smiled on him, and the word went round in a whisper, "I'll bet Kraushaar has sold one of his pictures." One evening Dolly suddenly appeared, begging the students not to give Sloan any more boxes of Tuscan cigars, for in his studio day after day he smoked like a chimney-stack and you could cut the smoke with a razor there. These Tuscan cigars were wrecking John Sloan's health. Now the students had had trouble finding presents that he liked, for he already had cuff-links that pleased him and he did not want even the most splendid of belts, though he treasured one gift, a two-volume work on Rembrandt; and they knew he preferred these Italian cigars with their red, white and green bands to all the Perfectos and Imperfectos of Cuba. But they sorrowfully promised Dolly to give him no more.

The Sloan class, according to Easoni Martino, was the noisiest in the annals of the League, but only on Johnny's off-nights, for when he was present the students scarcely dared to scratch their heads. One night he came in with a handful of tickets for a free show in the Village that Dolly had given him to distribute to them,—so that the poor actors would at least know that they were not playing to empty seats,—and a few evenings later, when the model was uninspiring, they thought they would play hookey and use the tickets. So, leaving a few of the pluggers behind, they started out six abreast only to observe the "Professor" coming towards them, whereupon, seeing beside them an automobile show-window, they wheeled and pressed their noses against the pane. Sloan walked straight on without a word. The play was good but between the acts they looked at one another and the girls giggled, "Do you think he recognized us?" while Martino said, "He isn't blind" and O. Soglow remarked, "What the hell. It isn't our fault. Who gave us the tickets?" As a rule, at 10:30, coming out of the class, on Fifty-seventh Street, "We who formed his bodyguard," as Martino said, "would stop to see which way the wind was blowing," and, if it was blowing east, Sloan would head that way for a quiet walk down-town alone. On other nights he would head towards Broadway, saying, "Don't you like to be in that human whirl? Don't you like to be in the stream of humanity?" Then they would plunge down Broadway when the crowds were swarming out of the theatres, pushing and shoving, Sloan always in front, bucking the tide, and all the others following, Indian file. Sometimes he would glance back to see how they were coming along, and Easoni Martino retained the impression of a group of swimmers, crossing Hell Gate, headed by John Sloan, an exhilarating bath in humanity, for him,—this devoted pupil felt,—whether battling with the Broadway tide or drifting with the current.

In his own studio some of the pupils saw another John Sloan, when the serious teacher began to cut capers or sing "Jolly Sixpence," accompanying this with appropriate dumb-show gestures. His voice was a basso-profundo and one of his pupils was convinced that he might have been a first-rate professional singer; but, however this may have been, there was no doubt about his impersonations,—when he mimicked Woodrow Wilson, for example. He would turn his face away and pass his hands lightly over it. Then he would turn again and there stood the austere president, smiling and bowing to right and left. Or he produced a pantomime of a distraught banker, getting wound up in ticker-tape while he was reading the news that his stock was rapidly disappearing. To the music of Ravel's "Bolero," Sloan acted this out with an ever-increasing dervish-like momentum.

CHAPTER XI

# SANTA FÉ

SLOAN WAS CONVINCED that he did not like "art colonies," although, as a rule, he chose to live in one,—remaining, wherever he was, detached and aloof,—and, moving between Chelsea and Greenwich Village when he was in the city, he only abandoned Gloucester for Santa Fé. His five summers at Gloucester were very rewarding, for he produced there some of his finest landscapes and small-town-life scenes, and with Randall Davey and Stuart Davis among his few friends there he had happy hours when the day's work was done. He recalled with special pleasure a party that lasted from sunset to sunrise, starting with a clam-bake and ending with breakfast on the rocks, but he said there was an artist's shadow beside every cow in Gloucester and the cows themselves were dying from eating paint-rags. He began to understand the natives who called the summer people "summer vermin." He repeated, "I don't like art colonies and I get out of them as soon as I hear there is one around me." Yet he never went more than five or six miles away, and when he turned his back on the Cape Anne colony he went to another colony in the Southwest. In this ambivalence he was like many artists.

At Gloucester, Randall Davey was also growing restless

in 1919,—Sloan's fifth summer,—and he proposed that, with their wives, they should go on a long motor trip in Davey's old chain-drive Simplex racing car. Davey had acted as Henri's assistant in managing summer classes abroad, and Henri, who had lived in Spain, Holland and Ireland, had visited Santa Fé three or four times and said it was the finest place in the world to paint. Like Davey, Sloan was still personally devoted to the master from whom he had diverged and who said that the Santa Fé climate was the best he knew; so the four were glad to set out with tents, a camping outfit and duffle-bags for the land of cottonwoods and sunshine. Travelling at seventy miles an hour, the Simplex, Sloan recorded, "made a noise like a soul on its way to hell"; but the Sloans and the Daveys fell in love with Santa Fé at once and Davey instantly bought a ranch and house there. A type of a "vanishing breed of artist—the man who paints for himself," while he "loves living and people," as Sloan called him, Davey settled permanently in a canyon three miles from the town.

The following summer, Sloan bought a house in the Calle Garcia, an old adobe dwelling with an orchard and a garden that was bright during the warm months with twelve rose bushes and hollyhocks against the adobe wall. There were lilacs, peonies and poppies, with blossoms that were ten inches across, and copper dahlias later in the season, raspberry, gooseberry and currant bushes, rhubarb and asparagus plants, a grape arbour and even an herb garden. In the orchard there were apple-trees, apricots, peaches, plums and pear-trees that were heavy with russet pears in autumn. Through the soft feathery cedar-like foliage of a beautiful tamarack tree, one caught fine glimpses of the mountains from this garden, and, putting modern plumbing and a bathroom in the house, Sloan built a studio a hundred feet away. To remind him of earlier days, he had the table from the Charcoal Club that appeared in his etching, "Memory," of the Henris and the Sloans. The former owner was an old Frenchwoman who continued to live near by and who came in to weed and prune to help Sloan and Dolly, for she was still fond of the orchard and garden she had planted thirty years before and loved every leaf, fruit and flower in them. This Madame Martin was a great character with a scorn of money and a stern sense of right who had been a Communarde in 1871 and had fought three days in the streets of Paris, escaping from the vengeance of the bourgeoisie after the fall of the Commune and finding her way at last to Santa Fé. During the winter, when the Sloans were in New York, Giorgio Valdes looked after the house, turning up with his spade in the garden in the spring shards of Indian pottery, a skull, old cartridges and Civil War uniform buttons. A gentle Mexican, devoted to the Sloans, he drank too much when they were away and was found dead one night lying in a ditch.

From 1919 onward, Sloan, for more than thirty years, was to spend four months of the year in Santa Fé, either in this adobe house or in one he was later to build on a hill that was six miles out of town. He loved the country in the Southwest, the mesas, old mountains and "geometric" hills, with the desert forms, severe and clear, that helped him, as he said, to "work out principles of plastic design." The piñon trees dotted the scene with exciting textures, and the atmosphere in this high altitude was transparent and light so that one felt the reality of things in the distance. This world was not covered with "green mould the way Eastern landscape is" and a tree here, he said, "is like a lettuce," while the colour was endlessly beautiful and all entirely new to him after his years in Pennsylvania, New England and New York. He found the sky "most wonderful," whether it was filled with broken clouds or remained a great cloudless dome over the desert landscape, perhaps with snow on the clear-cut edges of the mountains; and, although October in the Rio Grande country had none of the oranges and splashing reds or the haziness that characterizes an Eastern autumn, it had its own magical yellows, positive and neutral. There, in painting landscapes, Sloan often thought of Thomas Moran, who had such a complete knowledge of the subject that he was called photographic but who, if he had distorted his trees, might have been called surrealist, while he had some tricks, no doubt,—like every other artist! Sloan had written to Henri, almost at once, in the summer of 1919, "I have thirteen canvases under way—all memory things. I have done nothing out doors. Contrary to my usual custom in Gloucester, I have made no work in the open. I see things, the life of Santa Fé, or landscape, and make them afterward from memory, and I think it is producing results. Some of the things seem more like 'works' and less like 'studies.' "

In time, Sloan was often to paint out of doors again, occasionally on motor trips through the New Mexico country, when he pictured the "Little Black Mesa," for instance, on the western side of the Rio Grande, after driving along the road beside the river. He drew up at a pleasant spot where there were birches and aspens together with an almost grassy sward. On another occasion, a picnic, he painted a yellow-green tree on the Los Alamos highway, and the well-known "Chama Running Red" was the fruit of an excursion when he said the stream looked like flowing tomato soup. It was actually carrying good red earth to the Rio Grande and down to the Gulf, and this was the picture that contained the "solitary horseman" who might have been the famous equestrian of so many old stories. But how many landscapes Sloan painted of the country roundabout Santa Fé, the "Road up the Canyon," the "Santa Fé Sunset," the "Picnic, Arroyo Hondo,"—the picture of a holiday lunch five miles from the town,—the "Coyote Mesa," his own name for this rise of ground, the "Sunlit Peak, Santa Fé Canyon," the "Chimayo Country." This was the picture with the horses fording the river. Among numbers of others were the "Little Ranch House," painted in 1926, and "Bathers in the Acequia" of the same year, representing "two artists' wives" and a little boy taking a bath in an irrigation ditch north of Santa Fé. At one time or another, Sloan visited the Cowboys' Reunion at Las Vegas and the old turquoise mines near Cerillos, driving through little Mexican towns on the way, and the church at Guadalupe, which he painted with the moonlight and the tree silhouetted against the evening sky. Then he drove up to Taos where D. H. Lawrence's ashes were to rest in a chapel under tall pines on the top of Mount Lobo but where Sloan felt there were so many artists he could never have lived himself there with the kind of detachment he found so important. No one who saw his New Mexico landscapes could have wondered at his feeling that he should have been better known as a landscape painter.

As the years went on, he felt more and more the beauty of this country, and he was to write to Henri in 1925, "Love for it has sprung up in place of surprise." But, with all his interest in the natural scene, he still cared more for people, and he found in Santa Fé many subjects of the sort he had painted in his early pictures of the sidewalks of New York. He delighted in the old adobe houses, the crooked streets, the churches, the tall poplars, the cathedral in the brilliant sunshine, though he noted that strong sunlight was neutralizing and that in the New Mexico light the streets of the city were curiously grey. The plaza had some of the appeal for him that Madison Square had had in New York and he painted scenes of it at noon and in the evening with the promenade concert and young people strolling about or sitting on the benches. In another picture of the Alameda he showed the snow-like effect of the drifting seed filaments of the cottonwood trees, and he represented a "Hotel Dance," a "Travelling Carnival" and various parades that paralleled similar scenes in his New York pictures. The Corpus Christi procession and the Eve of Saint Francis procession,—leaving the cathedral at night,—were two of these, while in many other pictures Sloan recorded his impressions of New Mexico types, black-shawled matrons, young girls and mothers and daughters. In one, five devout women escorted from the cathedral the gold-fringed banner of the Virgin. The "Old Portale" was a picture of life on the ancient roofed sidewalk that survived from an earlier Santa Fé, and another survival that fascinated Sloan was the primitive process of threshing which was still visible in the town when he first arrived there. Sometimes a herd of goats were driven in circular stampede around a level floor of sun-baked mud; sometimes burros moved round the threshing floor. Sloan pictured both the burros and the goats at work.

For several years after he first arrived, Sloan spent a good deal of time designing floats and costumes for the annual Fiesta, and he took an active part in making them as well, saying it amused him to solve the problems of construction. But, while he had a few good friends, he did not "go around," he said, with the artists in Santa Fé, generally speaking, alert as he was to the life of the town and even more, perhaps, to the Indian life of the pueblos in the surrounding country.* Sloan was enthralled by the Indians and their dances and art, partly because he had recently awakened to a sense of the value of tradition and a deeper sense of the problems of aesthetic form. The Indians, he saw at once, had a great traditional base and worked together like the unknown artists who were inspired by a communal feeling in Gothic times, but the idea of such a thing had previously been abstract with him,—he had never encountered a living aesthetic tradition. To find it in his own country was a great surprise to him and his teaching presently reflected the idea, though, never thinking that Ameri-

* Up to this time, Sloan had known little or nothing of the American Indians. His diary of 1910 contains this entry: "With [Rollin] Kirby at about noon time to a 'moving picture' show—a feature that interested me was an Indian in full war bonnet of feathers and complete get-up who gave, in his broken English, a lecture. I had never before heard an Indian speak, so that his accent and pronunciation were new to me."

can artists should try to take over the Indian tradition, he said they must "push on in their own individualistic way." Sloan did not pretend to understand the Indian mind and he distrusted people who talked much about it, although he was impressed by John Collier's thinking and writing and staunchly supported this commissioner in all his undertakings; but his realization of the importance of tradition, seeing it at first hand, "slowed down," as some of his friends said, his socialistic hopes. He was excited at the same time by the boldness of the Amerindian art,—he liked this word Amerindian, which was coming into use,—by its primitive directness, its virile note and its versatility in the employment alike of line and colour. Struck at once by the coalescence of art and religion in Indian culture, he was convinced that the Indian pottery, to speak of one type of work alone, was better than most of the paintings of American artists.

In time, Sloan became deeply involved in the question of fostering the Indian arts, protecting them and forwarding the interests of the Indian artists, while almost from the first he began to study, for his own work as a painter, the ceremonies and dances at various pueblos. He was a devotee of dancing as Angna Enters practised it and, still more, Isadora Duncan, and he had been greatly impressed by a group of Chinese dancers in New York who appeared with the actor Mei Lang-Fang. He found the "little hesitation . . . very mysterious," he wrote, when they started the gesture just after the beat, while he marvelled at the way one entered at once into the Chinese tradition, not noticing that the women's parts were taken by men. Painting the dancer

Grace Emerson, he noted how earnestly she worked to help him catch the movements in the "beautiful sequence," as, later in life, he was to respond to the art of Martha Graham, which had, he said, "dignity and power and beauty." * But, as for Isadora Duncan, he said no painting could ever express the "adoration" that he felt for her, this woman who "lifted human movement to the level of the divine," as Sloan wrote later in *Gist of Art*. He spoke in his diary again and again of the "ecstatic enjoyment" her beautiful work had always given him, saying that she was "a symbol of human animal happiness as it should be, free from the unnatural trammels . . . not angelic, not super-human, but the greatest human love of life." With "her great thighs, her small head and full solid loins and belly," she "danced away civilizations tainted with brain vapours" and left all "human and holy"; and, in short, for Sloan, her dances were "the great thing of the day and the year," beyond all possible expression in words or in paint.†

* "I was agreeably surprised to find the work of herself and company so very satisfying, particularly in a new episode 'Night Journey' on the Œdipus theme. This had dignity and power and beauty. A sensuousness that I responded to. I feel sure M.G. is an important creative artist and am so glad that I was enabled to see her in her full maturity."—Diary, 1948.

The following year, in 1949, Sloan met at dinner the older dancer Ruth St. Denis and her dance-partner Ted Shawn. "We enjoyed the evening," Sloan wrote. "Shawn told of a special dance of native Australians arranged by authorities for his benefit. Very primitive but with great and varied artistry."

† Sloan repeatedly painted, drew and etched Isadora Duncan. Between 1908 and 1911 he met her a number of times, and she sent him tickets for her performances in Carnegie Hall. He was also her guest in a box at a performance of Maeterlinck's *The Blue Bird,* which he called "a piece of sentimentalism for the most part," and

So, caring as he did for the art of the dance, in many forms and of many types, Sloan was drawn naturally to the Indian ceremonial dances, and the first time he saw the Corn Dance at Santo Domingo he recalled Isadora Duncan. "I felt," he wrote in his introduction to a book by Ira Moskowitz, "the same strong emotion for the rhythm of the drums and primitive intensity of that age-old dance ritual that I experienced when I saw Isadora Duncan fill the stage . . . with her great personality." On this occasion he climbed up to the roof of an adobe to make sketches for the painting that he executed later, and, as a dust storm blew up, the Indians were a strange spectacle dancing half obscured in the flying clouds of dust. This was perhaps the "dream picture" with the "dancing phantoms" to which J. B. Yeats referred in a paper in the *Freeman,*—with "the light a dusky glare cast by a hot sun piercing through clouds," though it may have

---

he described a meeting with her in company with Glackens, Shinn, Lloyd Osbourne, the Henris and Ben Ali Haggin. On this occasion, she was "reclining on a large divan . . . not in the ordinary sense handsome. A light blue draped Greek sort of gown, plain dark hair and a fillet."

In his diary, 1910, Sloan wrote of her dancing, "It's hard to set down how much I enjoyed this performance. Isadora as she appears on that big simple stage seems like *all* womanhood—she looms big as the mother of the race. A heavy solid figure, large columnar legs, a solid high belly, breasts not too full and her head seems to be no more important than it should be to give the body the chief place. In one of the dances she was absolutely nude save for a thin gauze drapery hanging from the shoulders. In none was she much clothed, simple filmy coverings usually with a loin cloth."

In one of his notes, Sloan said, "I improvised a dance with Isadora, —nearly fell to the floor catching her." This was at "one of her committee meetings," as he told Raymond Duncan when the two met in 1949.

been "Koshare," another painting of a preliminary dance that preceded the Corn Dance at the pueblo. The Koshare was a reënactment of an ancient ceremony in which the ancestral spirits were supposed to be consulting, while they scanned the points of the compass for enemies in the distance, their bodies being covered with white clay and striped with black and red earth. Sloan also painted the mass that took place before the dance in the church at Santo Domingo, —about forty miles southwest of Santa Fé,—painting as well the Rain Dance at Cochiti, the most intimately picturesque of the pueblo dances. Another of his paintings represented the young men of San Ildefonso pueblo,—in still another Corn Dance,—followed by their wives, and in two of his well-known canvases appeared the "Eagles" of Tesuque, a pueblo that was only nine miles from Santa Fé. Tesuque preserved in large measure the native Indian atmosphere, and it augured well for the possibility of the Indians maintaining their own culture in the machine age. Sloan felt that the Eagle Dance displayed at its best the Indians' deep sense of harmony with all nature. Elsewhere, in a picture called "Grotesques," he showed a line of tourists watching another line of Indian dancers. The Indians, of course, were the grotesques, from the tourists' point of view, but for Sloan the shoe was on the other foot.

Many years later, Sloan recalled the "urge" he had felt to paint these scenes, and he related how he had given his own version of the Eagle Dance to break the ice at a party for some Indian guests. He said the Indians seemed to enjoy it and one old fellow came over to him and showed him that some of his gestures were not quite right. Once the

Sloans hitched up their Ford and drove to San Juan to see the Fiesta and the races there, the side-show catch-penny booths and the gathering of Indians, Mexicans and tourists at this beautifully coloured and elevated hilly pueblo. Then there was the game of El Gallo, an equestrian game which the Spaniards had played and which the Sloans witnessed at the Santo Domingo pueblo, with forty horsemen taking part while the women and the old men looked on from the roofs of their adobe houses. A rooster was hung by the legs between two sapling poles, and the Indians who upheld these jerked them away as the rider approached trying to clutch the bird in a wild dash. As ever, Sloan was captivated by the human appeal of the Indians, whom he painted in several pictures like "Better Mouse Traps," representing one of the shelters on the Albuquerque highway in which they displayed their pottery to the passers by. But it saddened him to feel that the Indians were an anomaly in the modern world because they lived the simple life of artists, and he marvelled that until recently their dance rituals and handicrafts had not been recognized as art. Their splendid water-jars and bowls, their pots and yucca-fibred mats had been relegated to natural-history museums and had only begun to be valued aesthetically as people came to understand the art of the Africans, Incas, Aztecs and Mayans. Sloan delighted in the Indian rugs, which he bought when they were still fifty cents, or even twenty-five cents, a figure, woven by women from the wool the men had sheared from their own sheep and dyed with vegetable dyes they had made themselves. He responded at once to the Indian modelling and carving, to the masks, pipes, dolls, bowls and baskets and the pots with designs in dull black on a polished black surface with patterns that were based on symbols of the life of the tribe. The designs, in some cases, went back four thousand years.

It was not necessary to understand an art in order to react to it, Sloan was convinced, and there may well have been much that he never understood in the Indian ceremonial and tribal life. But few could have been more sensitive to this art of the Southwest, the aesthetic work of the Indians in all its forms, among them the paintings in sand that had to be destroyed by sunset of the day during which they were made. He noted that the Indians had borrowed freely from the Spaniards and from other tribes, always assimilating these influences in their own design, but he saw that the new influences spreading from the tourist trade were rapidly affecting for the worse all these arts. The Indians, regarded as curios themselves, were asked to turn out souvenirs, bows and arrows, teapots, candlesticks, which, always in need of money, they were driven to produce, and the more interested Sloan became in the Indians and their life and art, the more he was concerned to shelter them. It touched him deeply that their work meant preparing the earth with seeds so that water and sun brought forth corn and wheat, while leisure with them meant thought of the gods, dance and song and the making of things which their minds asked them to make,—in a word, art. The Americans got much from them, but what could the Indians get from the Americans aside from silver dollars, for their jewelry, and paint?—and nothing could be worse for them than the touch of American commercial art or even of the serious art of the alien whites. A proof of this for Sloan was the work of the Kiowas of Oklahoma, which looked "like poster paint on kindergarten boards," with drawing, not Indian in character, which he described as "a cheap vaudeville treatment encouraged by tourists." He noted that the Indians had poor taste in contemporary art but were protected from this by their absorption in the past; and, feeling that the archæologists probably would not hurt them, he urged them to ignore the work of American artists.

In all this Sloan had especially in mind the young Indians who had turned away from the old decorative arts and were painting water-colours, evolving new forms from their tribal past that were based on the cultural symbols which had been used for centuries in decorating objects. The graphic work of the Indians had been largely confined to a picto-graph style and records painted on skins or incised on stone, but the ethnologist Dr. Edgar L. Hewett had encouraged the younger men to make water-colour drawings of their ritual dances. This was about 1915, and three boys of San Ildefonso, of whom Crescencio Martinez,—Ta-e,—was the first, had since produced finely stylized drawings, while the first to exhibit his work was Awa Tsireh, the son of the finest potter of the tribe. Other Indians of Tesuque also took up drawing and painting, followed by certain Hopis of Arizona. One could see in the old decorative work thc elements from which the painters derived, in this new departure of dancing and hunting pictures, just as the young men applied in their work the discipline of colour and line developed by their forbears in the useful arts. Sloan saw that they needed appreciation and seemed to droop without it, and he showed his own appreciation of what he regarded as their fine work, as early as 1920, in the most practical fashion. He took to New York with him to exhibit at the Independents show paintings by Awa Tsireh and Crescenzio Martinez. This was the first time that American Indian paintings had ever been exhibited as art.

## CHAPTER XII

# YEARS OF GROWTH

THE SOCIETY OF INDEPENDENT ARTISTS had been established in New York, for an annual exhibition, in 1917; and there, in two subsequent years, all thanks to John Sloan, the work of the American Indian artists appeared. The society had been organized mainly by Walter Pach, with the help of Walter Conrad Arensberg and Marcel Duchamp, and "with the purpose," as Sloan said in one of his notes, "of keeping an open door in American art." It permitted any artists, professional or not, to show a picture upon payment of a small entrance fee. Modelled on the French Society of Independent Artists and its policy, "No jury, no prizes," it was an outcome of Henri's efforts for the freedom of the artist from official interference, although Henri himself was at first not interested in it. For he was never enthusiastic about any projects which he had not initiated and directed himself, while the genuinely altruistic Sloan, who had no personal axes to grind, was always eager to work on behalf of other artists. The first exhibition, opening on the day on which America declared war, aroused the greatest possible popular interest, and twenty thousand visitors saw it during the first season. It interested Sloan himself to see what American artists would have to say about a world that was tumbling round their ears, and for him the show represented a composite of the soul of America with all its "amazing poverty" and "boundless richness." For the first year the president of the society was Glackens, but Sloan became the perpetual president in 1918, a position he was to hold for thirty-three years.

Always concerned for the Indians after he had gone to Santa Fé, Sloan was to become later, in 1931, the president of another society to forward their work, the Exposition of Indian Tribal Arts, so called, that remained for a number of years an institution in New York. Sloan's hope was to get the art of the Indians out of the museum, offsetting the demand of the tourist trade for knick-knacks and cheap curios while promoting native industries on the reservations; and the exhibition of 1931 was the first great showing of Indian art selected solely for its aesthetic value. A travelling exhibit was organized to win recognition for Indian artists in the important art-centres of the country, largely thanks to Sloan's Santa Fé friend, Miss Amelia Elizabeth White, who had sponsored and partly financed the whole undertaking. While Sloan wrote articles explaining and defending the Indian ceremonials and art, Miss White, of whom he painted one of his portraits, had asked Dolly Sloan to supervise the installation of the first show in the Grand Central Art Galleries in New York. Miss White then placed Dolly in charge of the Gallery of American Indian Art which she was to manage efficiently for several years. Sloan felt that some of the Indian paintings would make magnificent murals if they were enlarged, as they well might be, and he said that the Indians would soon learn how to cover any walls that were found for them and might form a school of American mural painting. Had not the Mexican artists already done so?

Proud as he was of his work for the Indians, Sloan was perhaps prouder still that the great Mexicans, Rivera and Orozco, had their first showing in the United States in 1920 at the Society of Independent Artists. Sloan was convinced, as he often said, that "below the Rio Grande is the only living nation of artists in the world today," meaning that the tendency of the Mexican people to appreciate graphic and plastic art was stronger than in any other modern country. He remarked in an interview once that Mexico was the best place for an artist to study now. He came to feel that the Mexican school was immensely beneficial to American artists and that this Latin-American-Indian strain might result in time in the formation of a distinctly American art. Feeling, meanwhile, that American artists could not take over the Indian tradition, he admired Rivera all the more because he was perpetually working to get closer to it, regarding Rivera himself as "the one artist on this continent who is in the class of the old masters." Admiring Orozco too, he felt that Rivera was the greater artist partly because his work had "beauty" * in it, while Orozco depended too much on dramatic effects. Orozco's forms were obviously "dynamic," but

* From about 1930, Sloan began to speak of "beauty," a term that he had disdained in earlier years. In fact, it became with him a cherished word, almost synonymous with "nobility" and "dignity." He used it in connection with the work of Bellini, Carpaccio and other old masters as well as with grandeur in the visible world. "But he always used the word," Helen Farr said, "for a concept to seek through the hard pathway of truth."

in Rivera, he said, there was "more classical harmony and thoughtfulness." It is possible that, at the end of his life, Sloan was drawn to Dartmouth College partly because of the Orozco frescoes there,* while for several hours he had watched Rivera painting his frescoes in the Workers' School in New York. He was struck by this painter's wonderful way of analyzing a human head and selecting the essentials of portraiture in it.†

Eager as Sloan always was to advance the work of other men, he might have been called philosophical in regard to his own, for he did little to promote the sale of his own pictures and painted solely, as he said, to please himself. Immensely industrious,—he painted more than a thousand pictures, aside from his etchings, lithographs, drawings and cartoons,—he called himself an amateur because he followed other means, illustrating and teaching, of making a living.‡

* Referring to these frescoes, he said in a note, "We who work in a money-seeking over-industrialized environment must eagerly draw on the artistic wealth of these Americans from below the Rio Grande . . . the masterly work of Rivera and the powerful designs of Orozco and other native Mexican painters, the most purely and truly American artists (excepting our own Indians) that are now at work on this continent."

† In his notes Sloan repeatedly referred to Rivera as "of the great line of the world's masters of art" and "the greatest living American painter." He said once in an interview, "Rivera is the only artist of the last two or three hundred years who belongs with the old masters."

Walter Pach, writing from Mexico City, where he was lecturing at the university (1942), passed on to Sloan a remark of Diego Rivera. He said he remembered Sloan's "canvas of girls under the Elevated" as having "more of New York in it" than anything else he knew.

‡ "I had to teach and do illustrations to pay the rent until I was over seventy—and I don't regret a day of it. I regard myself as an

The first painting he ever sold was a light-coloured recumbent nude with a pale apple-green scarf that Albert C. Barnes, his old school-mate, bought in 1913. At that time he was forty-two, and out of some four hundred he had made, many of which had been exhibited, he had sold only six paintings when he was fifty. "I have never been 'accepted,'" he said once. "I have never done anything anybody wanted," and he called it "a great day" when the National Gallery of Canada paid him $30 for lending it one of his pictures. In the nineteen-thirties he publicly offered to sell all the pictures he had on hand,—there were about eight hundred of them then,—for a guaranteed income of $100 a week, meaning, as a friend pointed out, that he would settle for the market value of one thousand loaves of bread a week. At a time when few American artists were more famous, he was glad to do a mural for a governmental project;* and later still he was willing to sell a painting for $75 to encourage the so-called Hall of Art. The theory of this institution was that low prices would create a demand for pictures both good and bad, but unhappily the manager found that bad pictures sold best and presently stopped taking any others. Meanwhile, the only pictures that Sloan painted for money were a very few commissioned portraits.† The first of these

---

amateur, and, if making a living at art is the criterion of the professional, Rembrandt was an amateur in his later years when he did his best work."—One of Sloan's notes, 1949.

* In the Bronxville, New York, post-office. The picture showed the arrival of the first mail-train in that town.

† Sloan painted many portraits that were not commissioned,—among them, several of himself and several of Dolly Sloan. Others were portraits of his friends. He painted, for instance, Horace Traubel, Gertrude Drick Smith ("Woe"), Will Shuster, the Santa

he had executed in 1911, when he went to Omaha to paint a German-American brewer with a "fine head," he wrote, and his kindly wife. He liked this quiet solid couple, but he had been "bashful at the idea" of attempting the portraits, he said, a feeling that dogged him again in his last commission.*

In later years Sloan felt that young artists were too much concerned with having their own one-man shows, saying that in his day no one expected such a thing until he was about forty-five. This had been his own age at the time of his first one-man show, the exhibition in 1916 that Mrs. Whitney gave him in the well-known Whitney Studio in Macdougal Alley. Gertrude Vanderbilt Whitney, later the founder of the Whitney Museum and long a friend of Henri and Arthur B. Davies, had bought four of the seven pictures that were sold at the exhibition of the "Eight" and had settled in the "Art Alley de Luxe" in 1907. A child of Edith Wharton's world, she had also taken an unprecedented step

---

Fé artist, Vagis the sculptor and William S. Walsh, the literary editor of the New York *Herald*. He also painted Edgar Varèse. In the background of his portrait of the latter he included the apparatus for electrically producing tonal vibrations that had been planned by this composer. Sloan painted as well David Dubinsky, the labour-leader, and his daughter.

Among Sloan's portrait etchings were those of his mother and Robert Henri (two), as well as the superb large plate of Paul de Kock, a composite of several contemporary portraits.

* When, in 1950, in his eightieth year, he painted a portrait of Arthur S. Meyer, the chairman of the New York State Board of Mediation. "He sits better than I paint," Sloan noted in his diary. After twelve sittings he was still dissatisfied with his "stumbling efforts" and he got the picture back the following year. With the excuse of varnishing it, he repainted it completely, apparently to the satisfaction of everyone concerned.

in becoming a sculptor herself and a friend of other artists, although she differed from Mrs. Wharton in seeing their problems at close range and possessing a warm-hearted wish to help them. For many years she covered the deficit of the annual Independent show while she worked for a better understanding of American art, giving exhibitions in her studio and presently buying in Eighth Street the buildings that were to house the new museum. She established this only after the Metropolitan Museum had refused her great collection of contemporary painters, many of whom she had sent to Paris, paying their hospital bills and aiding them in a hundred other ways. With a genuine personal enjoyment of artists and a love for the young and creative, she had also a great imaginative vision of the country, and, collecting the work of living artists, she encouraged research on the work of the past in a spirit that was wholly non-chauvinistic. She was more than assisted in all this by Juliana Force, who joined her as a secretary in 1914 and became the first director of the Whitney Museum.* Insepa-

* In its first two decades the Whitney Museum had regional and memorial shows and surveys of periods and schools of the American past. It had both one-man retrospections of living artists and one-man exhibitions of Feke, Earl, Rimmer, Homer, Ryder and Blakelock. In 1924, Mrs. Whitney backed Henry Schnakenberg's first of all shows of American folk art, then newly discovered, and the Whitney Museum also published monographs and books on American artists. Among these were Lloyd Goodrich's books on Eakins, Homer and John Sloan.

Mrs. Force herself was one of the first important collectors of American folk art.

At the time when he first knew her, Sloan painted a "sketch portrait" of Mrs. Force, which he reworked in 1949, making great improvements, he felt, in likeness and quality.

rable in retrospect, these two magnetic figures were symbols in their way of America's coming of age.

Sloan had been a member from the first of the Whitney Studio Club, and Mrs. Whitney bought three of his paintings, among them "Spring Rain," * and presented the "Haymarket" to the Brooklyn Museum.† For the rest, the exhibition at the Whitney Studio was presently followed by a larger New York show at the Hudson Guild, and thereafter Sloan, whose work had been often rejected,‡ was regularly exhibited in New York and elsewhere. Within a few years, meanwhile, largely as a result of the Armory Show, Sloan

---

He said of Mrs. Force that she was "probably the only person who tells Mrs. Whitney the truth, and I guess that is why she trusts her so."

* This was one of Sloan's favourites among his own pictures. Seeing it on the walls of the Whitney Museum, he said, "It comes into my consciousness not as a work of my own but like a fresh chord of music."

† The first of Sloan's pictures to be bought by a museum was "The Old Clown Making Up," acquired in 1919 by the Duncan Phillips Gallery in Washington. In 1921, the Metropolitan Museum bought "Dust Storm, Fifth Avenue." Later, the Boston Museum of Fine Arts bought "Pigeons" and the Wadsworth Athenæum at Hartford acquired the "Hairdresser's Window."

Regarding his "Pigeons," Sloan wrote to the director of the Boston Museum, "The pastime of raising pigeons was much in evidence in those days. The pigeons were flown daily for exercise [from the roofs that Sloan saw from his studio window] and also, incidentally, as a lure for stray pigeons from neighbouring flocks."

‡ Some of Sloan's paintings had been exhibited early, the "Old Walnut Street Theatre" in 1900 at the Chicago Art Institute and "Independence Square" at the Carnegie Institute in the same year. He was represented at the Pennsylvania Academy at every annual show between 1901-1907, and he was exhibited in New York in 1901 with Henri, Glackens and Alfred H. Maurer. It was after these years that his pictures were frequently rejected.

was to change the character of his work completely, as the originally intuitive painter gradually evolved into what might be called an intellectual painter. Never satisfied with his own work and discontented more and more with the consequences of Robert Henri's teaching, he said, "I never learned my trade," adding that just for this reason he was perpetually interested in solving new problems. He regretted that he had not been able to devote more time in his youth to the study of the traditional craft of painting, that he had to learn the hard way what every apprentice in the Renaissance had studied from the time when he was a child. Sloan recalled the phrase of Blake that J. B. Yeats had quoted, "A little flower is the labour of a thousand years," and, repudiating the spontaneity that Henri always praised, he gave up "direct painting" in 1928. Even as a young man he had cared more for "solidity" than the kind of surface "vitality" that Henri stood for, and he had come to feel that Henri's influence had led him to fight against his own natural tendencies in the eighteen-nineties. For in his early poster-style drawings he had been deeply concerned with the *design* that he was to teach his own pupils, and he was bent now on returning to fundamentals that he had then sought in a "two-dimensional way." It was this conviction that prompted Sloan, between 1928 and 1931, to develop an altogether new technique.

What started him seems to have been the feeling that he had done work in black and white,—in etching and charcoal drawing,—that was more "solid" than his painting, and, as he said, "I began to search for a way to paint in a technique that would offer the same procedure." How had he achieved with charcoal those "qualities of realization" which he was hoping to produce with paint? Partly by rubbing in a light drawing underneath which he then built up with more powerful linear work. This led to the idea of underpainting, to thinking about the under-form together with the enveloping colour-texture, the "under and over," the separateness of colour and form* which he was to find conspicuously in the painting of Renoir. For he said one could see the underpainting in Renoir's work better than one could see it in other artists because it was more "open,"—it was not painted over so much, so that one perceived the method there more clearly. At this time of Sloan's development, Renoir was the strongest influence upon him, and Renoir, more than anyone else, led him to examine the old masters and the methods of Van Eyck, Titian, Rembrandt and Rubens. He studied their technique in books by Max Doerner, Ralph Mayer and others, and later he said that the artist Paul Dougherty had told him a good deal about underpainting.†

Thus Sloan went back to the old system of monochromatic underpainting, in oil at first and in tempera‡ eighteen months later, isolating this, when it hardened, with gelatin, and glazing it afterwards to bring it to life with transparent

* Sloan liked the phrase of Hokusai expressing this duality,—"The principle of the thing and its colour skin."

He also remarked in a note: "Raoul Dufy floats the colour underneath and then floats the form on top. I like his work because it demonstrates so clearly the principle of separating form and colour."

† Two books that seem to have greatly interested Sloan at this time were A. P. Laurie's *Pigments and Mediums of the Old Masters* and Hans Hildebrandt's *The Problem of Form.*

‡ In one of his notes of this period, Sloan said, "Benton was telling me the other day about using tempera as an underpainting for oils."

and semi-opaque oil-varnish colours. He hoped by this means to transpose into colour the graphic significance, he said, of a richly textured charcoal drawing, achieving, as he put it, the "same brilliance and power," and his next step was to use occasionally the overglaze of coloured lines that came to be widely known as Sloan's "cross-hatching." Sloan disliked this phrase that was used with reference to his linear glaze technique because it distracted attention from his principle of using lines "to add realization to the form and colour statement." For this net of lines that lay over the form made it "tangible," he felt, and showed more positively where the surface was. Had not black pen lines on white paper always been accepted as a device for rendering form?—and Sloan could not understand why his openwork mesh seemed strange to people who were familiar with pen-work and etching.* He used his linear top-surface as a shell over the coloured form so that one could more readily see the understructure. Sometimes he used strong lines, sometimes they were comparatively mild, and actually he used this technical device almost as rarely in his later pictures as ash-cans had appeared in his earlier work. Yet just as he was tagged an "Ash-can" painter, so he was tagged with the phrase "Cross-hatching," catchwords that stuck to an artist and drew the minds of people away from anything like a serious appraisal of his work. Sloan also said that his lines, far from being always red, only seemed red in reproductions because of the limitations of colour-printing. In fact, they were all of dif-

* One of Sloan's reasons for liking Van Gogh was that he carried into painting the graphic line and texture of his pen drawings.

ferent neutral and semi-neutral hues, carefully chosen and varied in both value and colour.

Sloan went on experimenting with this "linear texture" to the end of his life, and he described the technique as "my way of abstracting," of "making the thing more real than it looks to the eye." The method pleased him because it was *not* like oil-paint brush-work and because the result did "not look as nature looks," for "works of art are made of wood and bronze and oil paint," he said, and should not look like flesh and blood. His charcoal drawings had made him happy because they "looked like bronzes" and this was the effect that he sought in his painting, saying, "I don't like a nude that looks too much like human flesh," preferring one that had a "dry hard look." In *Gist of Art* he added, "A good figure drawing is a 'living wooden image.' I sometimes tell students to make wooden Indians rather than to imitate the visual realism of flesh," and he said the most appreciative remark he had ever heard about one of his nudes was, quite simply, "She looks like metal." He felt a nude should be "sculptured with colour-textures, like a piece of bronze" or that it should have an effect of steel or brass, and, pointing out that Rembrandt's nudes had "no sensual quality," he detested Bouguereau's "vulgarity of cheap flesh." It pleased him when someone said that his nudes lacked the voluptuous charm of that "pornographic decorator,"—Boucher,—"for the boudoir trade," remarking that his own sole fear was that the flesh in his pictures might be "of the same colour that it is in nature." Loving the ribald robustness of Rowlandson and Hogarth, he said, "I hate those nasty lascivious nudes that people hang up in their houses . . . with bits of gauze drapery and slimy high-lights. I like a nude that is hard and firm, real as a work of art, so realized that you never think of it as a nude at all." *

This brought back J. B. Yeats's remark about the "Sloan woman" and her "quality of austerity and coldness," and it might be added that for models Sloan usually chose vigorous muscular women whom he painted, so to speak, as models rather than as women. He represented them lying on a couch, relaxing in a chair, standing before a mirror, stepping into a bathtub, and he usually added something to take away the effect of a pose and give the picture a look of ordinary life. He would put in the corner of a bed, a breakfast tray or a bowl of fruit, anything to escape from "those draperies hung on a screen"; but his figures were abstractions, nevertheless, and he sometimes used geometrical motifs or posed the model in the Z-shape as a theme. He recognized that in much of this work he was making "studies" rather than "pictures," and he said he lost interest in the end in etching because there he could do what he wanted to do, whereas, he said, "In painting I cannot do it."

* "Most nudes that people buy are what I call pornographic. They look as though the artist was in love with the model."—One of Sloan's notes.

Sloan especially disliked what he called the "mechanistic sensuality" of American advertisements and much American painting. He contrasted their "coarse" treatment of women with the "tenderness" of Forain's early work before this French artist became sentimental. He said, "Our attitude towards sex suggests a kind of dirty plumbing made superficially sanitary by the use of deodorants." Again contrasting all this with the "animal-humanism of Havelock Ellis," he said, "How seriously unhealthy are our vulgar beach costumes and brassière ads."

What he meant was that he felt he could never quite solve the problem of translating into colour the "graphic vigour of the charcoal drawings and etchings,"—among them the figure etchings of which he made thirty-one during the years 1930-1933. He had seriously taken to painting nudes when he began to teach at the League to keep "a couple of pages" ahead of his pupils, but his period of sustained interest in the nude figure had begun in 1931. He called it "the most difficult and noble problem which has interested the artists of all ages, today considered 'finished' by the fashion experts."

Perhaps Sloan's feeling in regard to flesh called for a little explaining in view of his delight in Renoir, that lover of flesh, and so did his feeling in regard to colour in which he often said that he was not interested at all. He meant "colour in itself" but he kept repeating in his notes, "Colour isn't anything important in a painting. Form, arrived at through mental experience derived from the sense of touch,—that is fundamental. Colour is just an extra." Guy Pène du Bois observed that Sloan never painted anything because he was moved by the beauty of its colour,—that he was never stirred, for instance, by flowers; yet he could not have been a painter if colour had not meant much to him, and some of his notes were illuminating in this connection:

> An artist [for instance] is really a brain floating in a world of colour. He has to accomplish the feat of making 'thing concepts' while he is floating in this colour, yet with brain and memory.
>
> The eyes are just instruments through which colour documents are sent to the brain where "things are made."

Moreover, Sloan was shocked to hear a young artist say that he was pleased by the colour in some moving-picture films. He said many young artists brought up in the ultra-modern movement never looked at nature any more, and, as they never got colour ideas from nature, they did not know the difference between the true and the false. All this indicated, on Sloan's part, a very marked interest in colour, and so did his observation that in "black and white photo projections" he was often strongly conscious of colour. It was, he said, "real colour, although very subtle," and he had noted this "strange fact" again and again. Incidentally, for several years, he had found great joy, he said, in the Maratta system of producing paints. Hardesty Maratta put up in tubes regulated colours, twelve colours of full intensity, twelve bi-colours and twelve hues, and Sloan felt that some formulated schemes for using these orderly pigments gave the painter a reliable instrument, "like a tuned piano." Sloan used these paints in his Gloucester landscapes and in some of his city scenes, and he only gave up using them because, after Maratta died, he felt they were no longer made so well.

The Maratta system had helped Sloan to enlarge his palette in the Gloucester days and develop what he called the "orchestral" colours with which, in the twenties and early thirties, after he had ceased to paint "Sloans," he returned with renewed zest and power to the New York setting.* It was during these years that he painted "Jefferson Market, Sixth Avenue," the "Grand Central Station," the

* Sloan contrasted the "orchestral colours" of his later work with what he called his earlier "fife and drum colours."

THE PICNIC GROUND, 1906

WAKE OF THE
FERRY, No. 2, 1907

THE HAY-
MARKET, 1907

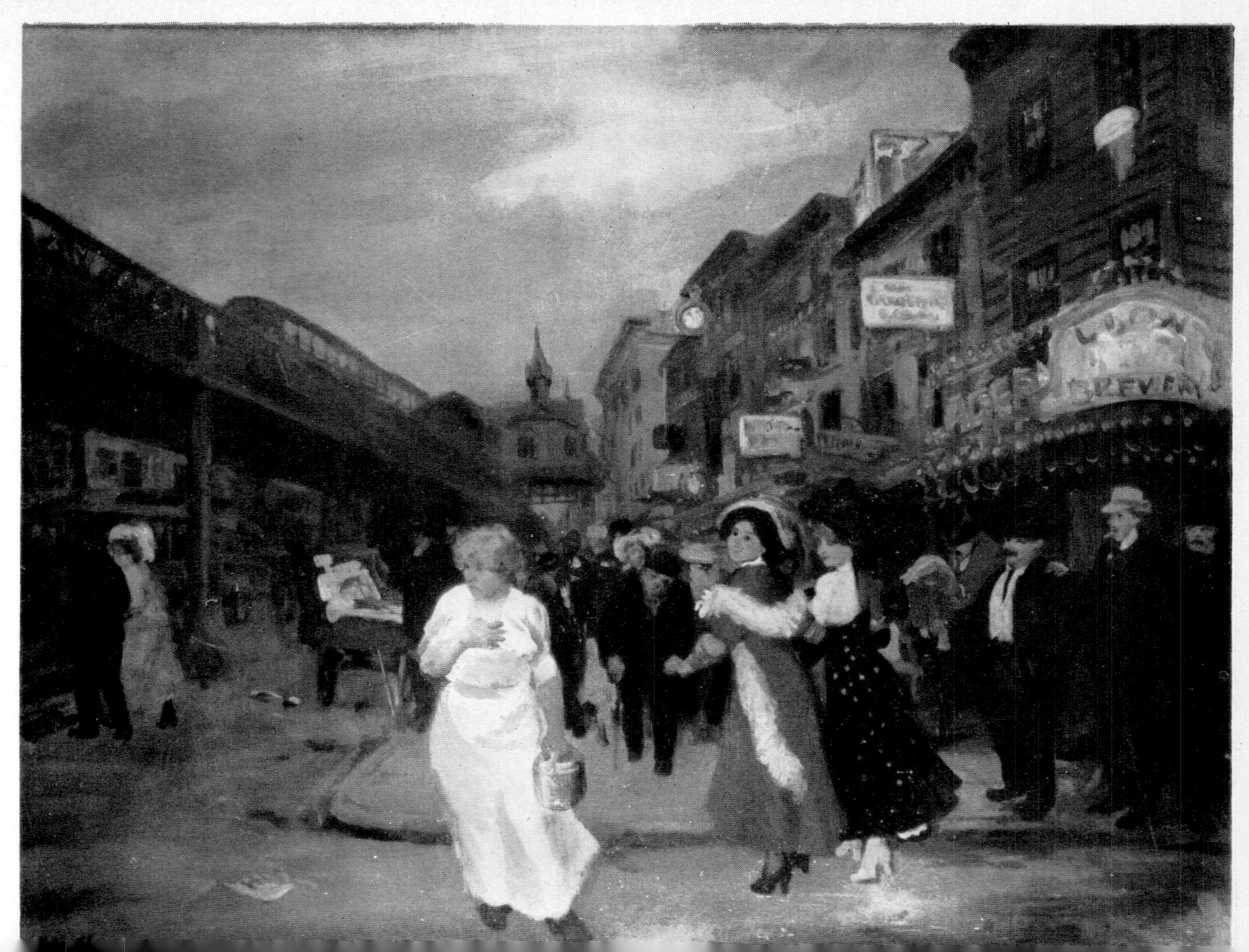

SIXTH AVENUE
AND
THIRTEENTH
STREET, 1907

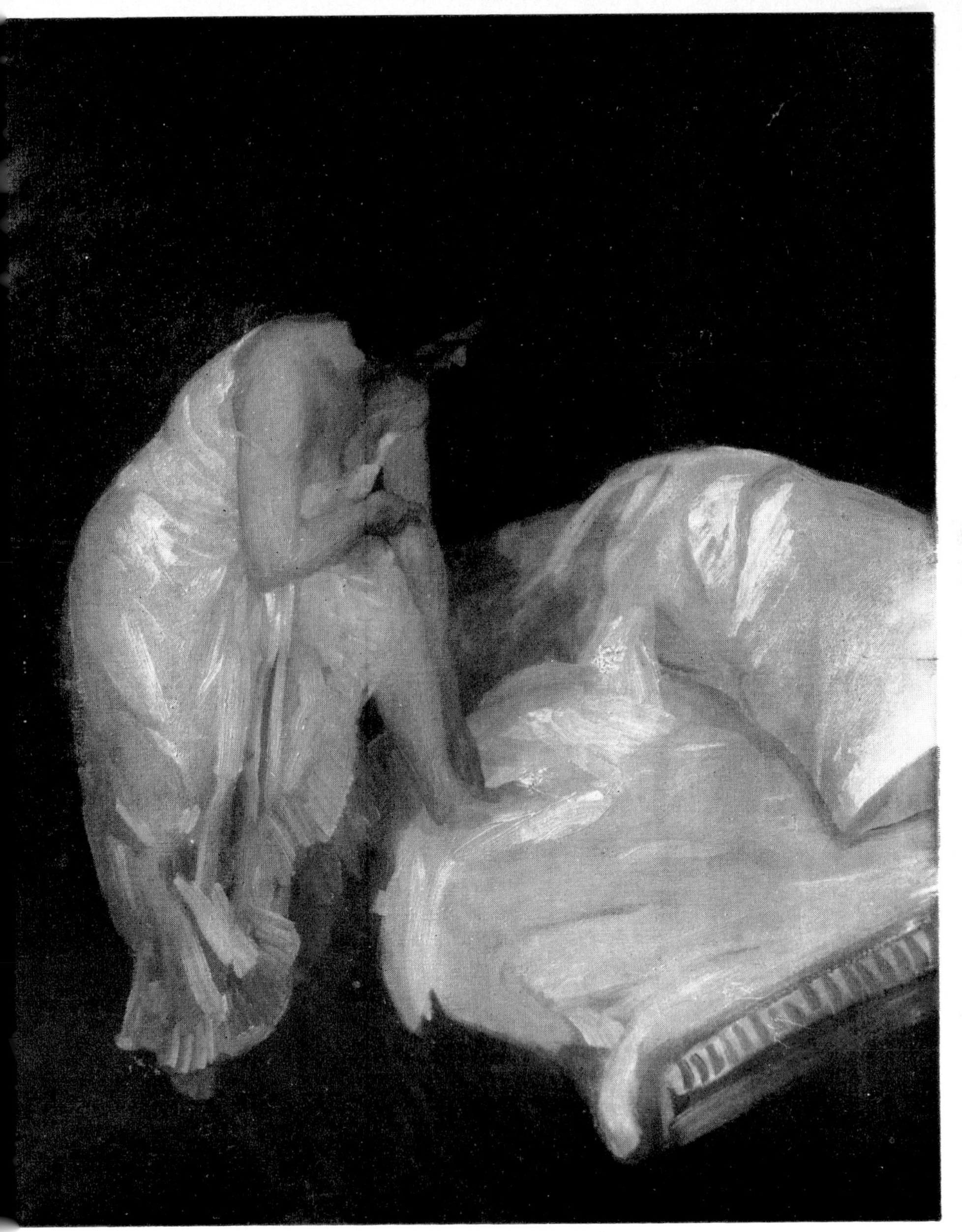

THE COT, 1907

KENT CRANE, 1907

CHINESE
RESTAURANT, 1909

PIGEONS, 1910

WOMAN'S WORK, 1911

McSORLEY'S
BAR, 1912

McSORLEY'S
BACK ROOM, 1912

HILL,
MAIN STREET,
GLOUCESTER, 1916

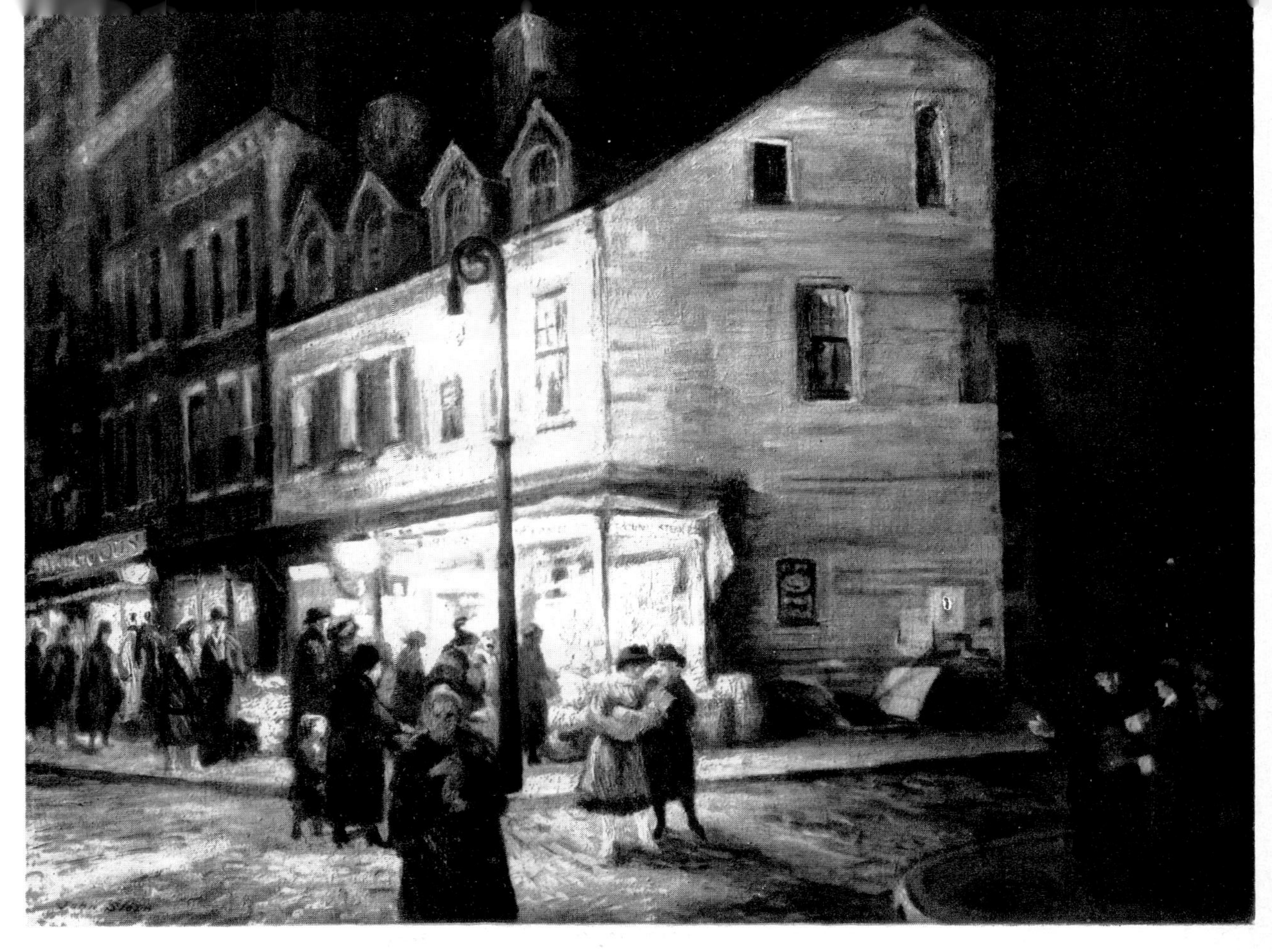

BLEECKER
STREET
SATURDAY
NIGHT, 1918

LAFAYETTE
HOTEL, 1927

CHAMA
RUNNING
RED, 1927

NUDE ON THE ROOF, 1936

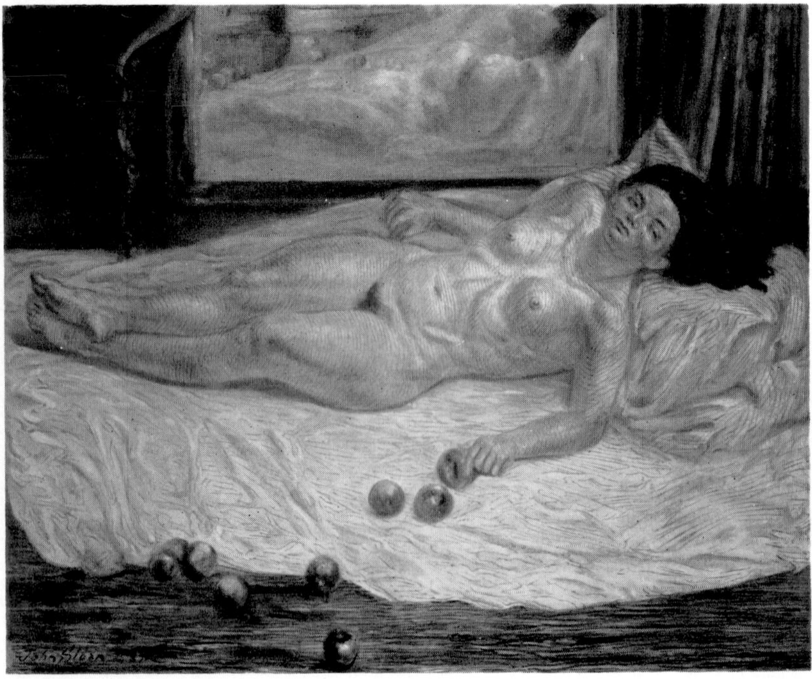

NUDE AND NINE APPLES, 1937

"Lafayette Hotel," * "Sixth Avenue and Third Street," "Old Tammany Hall" and "The City from Greenwich Village" with the lighted office buildings looming in the distance. He had always been interested in the elevated trains bending round a curve with the lights flashing from the windows of the cars,—a scene that he presented in two of his pictures, —and a sudden impulse led him out one snowy winter night to study Broadway with its gay illuminations. He went out in the cold and stood with pencil clutched in petrified fingers making memoranda for "The White Way." He also spent the summer in New York in 1933,—the only summer so spent in twenty-seven years,—in a big studio overlooking Washington Square from the South and the teeming life he recorded in other pictures. Some of these were larger pictures than the earlier Sloans had been, as they were more complex and better composed, with more design and much more colour, while they were less records of incidents than great panoramas or tableaus that celebrated the pageantry of the city. They were "more sculptural" and "less emotional," Sloan said himself, but they expressed with greater intensity the note of the artist's earlier work and his old romantic feeling for New York.

* In 1928 a fund was collected to present this picture to the Metropolitan Museum. Sloan made an etching of the old Lafayette, that favourite resort of artists and writers, and presented a print to every contributor to the fund.

CHAPTER XIII

# CHARACTERISTICS

DURING HIS FORTY-SIX YEARS in New York, Sloan occupied several studios, beginning in the Sherwood building and the garret in West Twenty-third Street and ending in the Hotel Chelsea a few blocks away. At various times he also lived in Fourth Street, Perry Street and Washington Place and at the Hotel Judson in Washington Square. For three or four years he had a studio at 35 Sixth Avenue, a loft that was partitioned off from a knitting factory and that had eight windows to the northwest. Only a little sun entered late in the afternoon and this gave him no trouble, while the light pleased him. He noted in his diary that some Italians who worked in the building had bored holes in the studio walls,—"to see the artist and his model. Oh, thrilling!"

In the diary, which he called "this plain dull true story of a living," Sloan referred to several of his models, one of them Miss B., a "tall narrow girl" with heavy-lidded eyes and a long upper lip. She was not pretty, Sloan wrote, "but I felt that there was a very interesting point of view to be taken of her." There was Emma Pardo, the little Spanish model, and a Bohemian girl who came in one day and whom he painted nude on the edge of the cot; and there was a Negro girl apropos of whom he said that the Negroes were well termed "coloured people." For it struck him that they furnished the most beautiful individuals of all the racial strains in this country.* Then there was the charming Japanese Waki Kaji, who posed for Henri and Glackens too and had written two novels of the blood-curdling type and said that her mother's mother was "one of the Whitneys." Above all, there was Yolande, whom he painted singing, painting her indeed again and again,—once smiling, with a note of paper in her hand and a low-cut open bosom,—and whom he described as "a bright nervous bird-like young lady." In 1909, when he first saw her, she was only seventeen, but she was to turn up again in 1946, still the gay, lively, highstrung girl that she had been thirty-seven years before, although she had survived four husbands and was ready for a fifth. He had painted her four times at first and he now painted her twice again, saying that she was "the world's most difficult subject." Still like a wild bird, she kept up her sprightly flow of talk, with her spirited face in almost ceaseless motion.

Another of Sloan's models was a strange little red-haired socialist girl who bombarded him with letters for four or five months, addressing him as "Sir Hildebrand," she being the damsel in distress and he the knight who had come to her rescue. Jennie D. called herself "Cyrana, the feminine of Cyrano," the "young woman who loved a bright particular star," and she told Sloan that he was the "most disturbing and painful influence" that had ever come into her life. He had captured her imagination and roused in her feelings

* Sloan detested what he called the "filthy tide of race prejudice."

and desires of which she had been scarcely aware until she met him, for he was different from anyone she had known, lived or worked with in her uncertain, confined, precarious life. With various ambitions to enter a convent, lead the unemployed or accelerate the social revolution, she was connected with a suffrage campaign committee, but, aspiring to be a novelist, she poured out her feelings in letters to Sloan that suggested another Marie Bashkirtseff. He gave her stories of Maxim Gorky, but he wrote in his diary that he could not "respond," being, as he said, "too selfish to want any disturbance," and he was probably relieved when he left town for the summer and the correspondence ended. He said that Jennie's strangeness frightened him. As for her, she was "going back to the shadows" from which she had emerged, she wrote, shadows that were denser because she had "seen the light."

Thirty-five years later, happening on these letters again, Sloan said they embarrassed him so much that he had scarcely read them, and he had kept them in a package "with a copper plate as a disguise" in order that Dolly might not find and read them. Dolly would have misunderstood the situation. He added in 1950, "It affects me today like an uncovered crime of the past." At that time one of his constant models was a charming witty woman who had danced with Pavlova in the Russian ballet but who had broken her hip and developed a fear of falling that was fatal for a dancer. Her sheer beauty, however, was wonderful, Sloan wrote again and again, she had an "overpowering" beauty of figure, and Charlotte L. was spirited and enthusiastic too, a quality that always raised Sloan's own spirits. He had found that it made a great difference to him to work with good professional models, although not all of his models were charming or young; but, as he once observed, "Who cares for youth and beauty in art? You can see it any day at five-thirty coming out of Saks or Macy's." One model who had interested him was an old woman who described herself as a "laundress for gentlemen mostly" and who also said that in her time she had posed for Winslow Homer and E. A. Abbey. She had been painted by Winslow Homer on the roof of his studio building as a young lady coming from a dip at the seaside, and, having good colour still, she was bright-eyed and spry.

Another whom Sloan especially liked was Zenka Stein, a Czech, whom he called "the best professional model in New York," a kind, hearty woman, extremely paintable, an expert craftswoman in raffia, who posed for several of his pictures. In one of these he painted her leaning against the etching-press in a dark corner of the room, and he greatly enjoyed Zenka Stein's ingenuousness and wisdom, not to speak of her wonderful broken English. But some of the older models were tragic figures. Once I went to see Sloan in his Sixth Avenue loft, and as the door opened a woman came out with bedraggled ostrich plumes and a generally dilapidated air. "Do you know who that was?" Sloan said, as he closed the door. "She is the daughter of ———," and he named a renowned American author, one of the most renowned, who had been famous the world over a generation before. I had often heard of her when she was a girl, and I knew that her life had been very unhappy, but Sloan said she had gone down too far to be useful as a model and only dropped in nowadays to ask him for a quarter.

It was to this Sixth Avenue loft that Theodore Dreiser came one day, eager to examine a studio for a novel he was writing, but he found none of the atmosphere that he was looking for in this bare, prosaic, unromantic workroom. As Sloan put it, Dreiser "saw at a glance that I was not leading the right kind of artist-life for his purposes: no rich furnishings and none of the typical trappings like fish-nets and spinning-wheels which were the earmarks of the 'studio.'" In Dreiser's *The "Genius,"* when it finally appeared, one saw what he was looking for, church candlesticks, tapestries, bits of old silver and brass, Flemish and Venetian tables and chairs and a fish-net dyed green and spangled with fragments of a mirror to look like scales. He must have found some of these later in Everett Shinn's studio, for Shinn liked these trappings and Dreiser said that in drawing Eugene Witla's character he had Shinn in mind,—although no one who knew Shinn would ever have guessed it; but certainly in describing Witla's pictures he was thinking of the "Ash-can" school, Luks's work, and Shinn's, but especially Sloan's. He showed how shocking the public had found these pictures of tenement harridans, pan-handlers, rag-pickers and sandwich-men, phases of life that were supposed to be beyond the pale of artistic significance because they were so "commonplace or customary." Yet, grim and shabby as the scenes were, the pictures were somehow touched, the author of the novel said, with romance and beauty. Sloan noted that

Dreiser referred to his own "Dust Storm" and "Pigeons," but many of Witla's pictures might have been his, scenes of crowds pouring from the theatres at night, Greeley Square in a drizzling rain, street-lamps relieving black shadows of people and sky. In others whitish-grey plumes of smoke rose from rickety chimney-stacks under a sky lowering with blackish-grey clouds, and there was the famous Sixth Avenue restaurant seen through the Elevated track with a driving rain pouring between the interstices of light. All seemed to shout, Dreiser said, "I'm dirty, I'm commonplace, I am grim, I am shabby but I am life!"

If Sloan had read the book with sympathy and care, he would have seen that, in celebrating Witla, Dreiser was in reality celebrating him, but he had only scorn for this "ex-novelist—I think he's 'ex' "—who was editing the *Delineator* at the moment. He said later that *The "Genius"* was "so banal and sentimental and saccharine" that he could not understand how Dreiser was considered, or had been considered, the "Hemingway of his time," and that it was fantastic to describe "some of my pictures as the work of that fictitious and impossible artist." How could Dreiser have presented that kind of work as selling successfully in the artist's youth and moreover at the time when it was painted? —although Sloan might have recognized the reality of Dreiser's picture of the dealer who "spoke English almost more than perfectly" in his red-velvet gallery. But no, Sloan would have none of this book* and he contrasted *The "Gen-*

* Feeling that *The "Genius"* did not ring true to the artist life of the time, Sloan disliked the taste for luxury that Dreiser showed in

*ius*" with Joyce Cary's *The Horse's Mouth,* which he was reading at the time with great interest and liking, finding it a "far more true and loving real picture of an artist" and seeing in Gulley Jimson a "George Luks type." This ribald romantic tippler delighted him and he said the book was full of "English robust earthy healthy humour," the kind he had loved in Fielding, as in Rabelais and Balzac. It outraged him that this tragic story was advertised in America as comic.

In those after days, speaking of the "Eight," Sloan said that they had kept away "from the social veneer side of life. Instead of painting powder-puffs, we painted brooms," and he had preferred the scenes where brooms were in evidence, —if not often used,—not that he idealized poverty for others or himself. He had no desire whatever to live the hand-to-mouth life of the starving artist,—any more than he wished to be the kind that Dreiser liked,—and he believed in having an adequate studio, proper food and plain comforts with no unpaid debts. He found it embarrassing to borrow money and lived, in fact, by choice, the sober well-regulated bourgeois American way, as remote as possible from Gulley Jimson's, or still more from Goya's, but suggesting the way Van Gogh would have preferred to live. For Van Gogh longed, as he always said, to live a quiet life, enjoying a measure of happiness without too much sorrow, and he had never chosen the strange happenings that his personality seemed to invite. Sloan's habits were as temperate and simple as Mi-

---

this book. He also disliked Dreiser's carelessness about women whose hearts were wrecked by an "artist's" desire for "experience." On the other hand, he was deeply moved by *An American Tragedy,*—of which he "read every word,"—and he liked Dreiser's *Sister Carrie.*

chelangelo's, while he lacked the Florentine passion for worldly gain; and having, moreover, small means, he liked the idea of having small means as almost the token of being a serious artist. He would have agreed with Whistler's motto, "It is better to live on bread and cheese and paint beautiful things than to live like Dives and paint pot-boilers," and when he recorded in 1906, "Our assets reach $1200," he added that, in spite of liabilities, "we feel right solvent." Two years later he reckoned that his income for the year 1907 had been, on the average, $50 a week, and he asked for little else if there was money enough in the bank,—with a small reserve of savings,—for the year ahead.

For the rest, Sloan not only regarded "painting to sell" as unthinkable but he never thought of making a living by painting. Reading Pissarro's letters, he said it had always shocked him a little that these French artists expected to live by their pictures, that even Millet, who was so poor and had a large family to support, never dreamed of any other way of making a living. He took it for granted that his own way of keeping the wolf from the door was to carry on his work as an illustrator, and he was always inclined to suspect artists who had money or had rich clients as if this proved that they could not be the real thing. He was shocked by the signs of the opulence in which, for instance, Saint-Gaudens had lived when, years later, he visited Cornish, New Hampshire, and he had quietly slipped away after a brief visit to the Century Club, feeling that this comfortable repose was not for him. Here was "rest from the world and its riot" but it only made him realize that poverty was much more his dish of tea. Many American artists and writers have shared this conviction that was bred in Sloan by the too-insistent presence of a money-making world.

Frugal as, in a sense, he was, and above all perhaps austere, with little money to spend for any purpose, Sloan was generous to his fellow-artists, whose etchings and paintings he bought, as he had bought Glenn O. Coleman's drawings. He had acquired in this way, for example, O. Soglow's first etchings, as he bought one of Baylinson's paintings, saying it would make any soft spots of weakness in his own work stand out. He bought, and presented to the Brooklyn Museum, Philip Evergood's "The Old Wharf," the first of Evergood's paintings to be acquired by a museum,—encouraging the painter by this fraternal act,—as he presented to the Corcoran Gallery in Washington the portrait that Robert Henri had painted of him. To the Exposition of Indian Tribal Arts in Santa Fé he donated $500 in 1931, wishing to encourage gifts from the directors; and, incidentally, he bought for himself for $15 at an auction a picture of race-horses by Géricault. It was in bad condition but he liked the horses, not knowing that the picture was Géricault's work,—it was listed in the auction catalogue as by "Gerricanet"; and he refused for many years to sell it. In the end this picture went to the Smith College Museum.

One of Sloan's mottoes was, "Since we have to speak well of the dead, let's knock them while they are still alive," and both on the platform and privately, in conversation or in his notes, he abounded in candid comments on other artists. It was well and generally known that he had small regard for tact,—in this resembling the Almighty, as he once remarked,—and he also said that he envied Voltaire more than anyone he knew for "keeping up that vitriolic mind." From "fossils" and "cabbage intellects" he suffered as much as any man,—as the hero of *The Horse's Mouth* suffered from the brave lads who had fought against every new movement from the Pre-Raphaelites down. These men resembled, Sloan might have observed, the American painter who said the police should have stopped the first Independents show, but Sloan stigmatized few of the older artists, well knowing that one could not "convince these people" * and might therefore just as well ignore them. With some, Alden Weir, for example, he had happy relations. He found Weir a "fine big hearty man" with a perennial youth that made him always good company, Sloan recorded, and he was struck by a "beautiful little thing of nudes in grey mist by a stream" that Weir was exhibiting at Montross's. With Weir, who came twice to his studio to see them,—as with Henry Ranger,—he said his own etchings were a "big success." †

Sloan reserved his vitriol for a few of his contemporaries, —the "Billy Sunday of art," for instance, as he called one painter whom for a number of years he had admired.‡ Dis-

* In his diary, 1908, Sloan spoke of discussing with George Luks the demerits of Will H. Low and Kenyon Cox: "I argued with him that he could never convince these people, they don't know great work when it is a contemporary product. They bow of course when the celebrated work of the old masters is before them, but that's merely educated into them—they don't really see it."

† The old sculptor Daniel Chester French wrote Sloan in 1926 a charmingly courteous letter. He said he had become the possessor of one of Sloan's pictures and hoped that this might lead to a personal acquaintance. "I wish you to know," said French, "how much I value the picture, both for itself and as an example of your work."

‡ In 1910 Sloan wrote in his diary, "Met Jonas Lie, painter and a good one." He did not record his later opinion of this artist, but

liking George Bellows, the "beloved disciple" whom Henri regarded as almost a son, he also found Georgia O'Keeffe's work distasteful, saying that she was "just like Bouguereau, for if you were to enlarge a Bouguereau toe it would be like one of her enlarged leaves. She blows up leaves, or lilies, and paints them in like an old lady copying a chromo." Elsewhere he said that Georgia O'Keeffe was "nothing but a sophisticated Grandma Moses," while of Grandma Moses herself he said that she was "an innocent little old lady who makes stumbling copies of Currier and Ives." What a farce that she should be exhibited in Europe as an American artist! Of John Taylor Arms, "a sort of father of our printmakers," Sloan said that he knew a great deal about etching and that technically his work was almost "supernatural" at times, but that, on the whole, this work was "very boring"; while he all but completely condemned Zuloaga and Sorolla, the Spanish painters who had such a vogue in New York. He said Zuloaga had set out to see things as Velasquez and Goya saw them rather than to see them for himself and Sorolla had "no philosophy expressed in paint." The Sorollas, he said, were "dashing and full of colour," but thin, loosely painted and essentially "clap-trap."

Sloan was respectful, however, to more artists than he censured and his taste was surprisingly catholic at the same time, for he liked certain painters whose work was poles apart from his,—Charles Demuth and the "very fine" and "original" John Marin. Having always admired Arthur

---

about a certain other contemporary he remarked, "He is just like a dead man dug up." Of Sargent, Sloan said that he "turns everything into satin."

B. Davies and Maurice Prendergast's "great works," he was drawn, personally at least, to Arthur Dove, a "very nice sort of young chap," he wrote on one occasion; and he was fond of Stuart Davis, the "ambitious eager young artist," his old friend's son whom he remembered in a baby-carriage. In those days Sloan and Edward Davis had ridden out of town on a big clumsy tricycle to make sketches. For the rest, Sloan had much to say in praise of Thomas Hart Benton, Ben Shahn, Marsden Hartley and Max Weber. He wrote once, "Benton's figures look as though they should be carved in wood and grouped around a crêche, American style," adding in a note, "I respect the man for doing what he wanted to . . . He has not sold out to changes in fashion." * His remarks on Marsden Hartley were generally favourable, though he said, "Hartley's mysticism is a little too much for me and I hope that it won't prove finally too much for his pictures." He was interested in Hartley's "broken colour Impressionism" and especially in two or three canvases of "the more sincere nervous sort";† while he said of Ben Shahn's

* "Benton puts a decoration on a room and the people ooze off the wall and their knuckles and kneecaps and wrinkles get into the room with the audience. Of course it proves that they are real and strong."

"The critics like Benton because he has a style. He always goes on making reliable Bentons. You can recognize them. You see the wrist and know his worm. The Benton worm gets started in the grass in the foreground, gets hold of the farmers and comes out in the smoke of the Benton locomotive. That connecting worm always goes on . . . It isn't the American scene that is good in a Benton, it is the mental response to a living world around him."—Sloan's unpublished notes.

† Sloan recorded in his diary in 1908 that Maurice Prendergast had sent Hartley to see him. Hartley brought with him some pictures that he had done in the Maine mountains. "Some of them

painting that it had a "powerful impact because there is emotion under mental control . . . It has mental importance," Sloan added, "bitter, and yet a kind of quality in the inter-relations of colour-areas that are not in themselves important." Referring to Kuniyoshi, he said, "His work is playful and thin but he uses much graphic technique with clever results." He thought more highly of Max Weber. Saying that his later things grew too careless with their "tiresome black graphic line," he remarked that Max Weber had great mastery of colour and that in his work "you always feel you are looking at *art*, art related to an ancient tradition." Another artist he admired was James Wilson Morrice, the "Canadian Prendergast," as he somewhere called him, adding, "I regard him as one of the greatest landscape painters of the time." Morrice gave him a small panel, a street scene in Paris, that Sloan always treasured and kept in his studio on the mantelpiece.

Of the French twentieth-century artists, Sloan, of course, had much to say, and his views about their work were far from simple, for, having small interest in work that was wholly abstract, he felt that he owed much to the "ultra-modern movement." But this, he said, was "for adults. It is a medicine for adults," observing that "the kids have raided the medicine closet," that "for those kids the medicines are drugs" and that in consequence "they are on a jag." He continued, "These little imitators are just going from the abstract to the abstruse to the absurd." As he said of Picasso, however, about whom he wrote repeatedly, he is "not an

---

seem affectations," said Sloan, "the clouds especially, like tinted buckwheat cakes. The work has, however, several good spots in it."

abstract artist, for all his work derives from contact with life at first hand or at second-hand from other works of art." He also said, "I think I have learned more from Picasso than most of his imitators. His value is not in what he does but in what he is thinking about . . . Picasso is a giant, a genius; his personality is unique and the time provided him with a happy hunting ground for his explorations." * Again, "Picasso slices away everything extraneous and shows the students only the very necessary bone and muscle structure of design." But Sloan's most interesting comment on Picasso involved a comparison with his own work. "As an artist," he said, "who went through the period of striving for 'character,' I admire Picasso's work for its absence of character, for the classic impersonal qualities it shows in the heads of the figures." Meanwhile, he said of Gauguin that he was "an outgrowth of the poster movement" and that "Braque takes all the stupidity out of still life." He said, "All Matisses are not Matisses. There are the real ones and then the wall-paper designs," adding, "Most of the abstract artists are misplaced interior decorators who have 'taste' in colour." This led him to say, "What is Mondrian but a designer of lino-

* "Picasso is amazing, like a display of fireworks; the pattern changes every few minutes and his public is trained to admire this virtuoso who can be classic in the morning and expressionist after tea time. He is like an archæologist who might fly by helicopter from site to site, exclaiming over Egypt and then New Guinea, plucking a shard here and a spear there and then exhibiting the results to a public too ignorant to recognize his disorganized procedure."

"Picasso has been working with dynamite. He leads the crew of wreckers who make the way for liberty. Picasso is a sign-post to the new Renaissance, but the sign-post is not the town."

Sloan once referred to Picasso's "Guernica" as "a giant's visiting card."

leum? I have a rug from Sears Roebuck that is more exciting aesthetically than any Mondrian I have ever seen, because it is richer in colour and has surface texture." *

Once Sloan said, "Artists, in a frontier society like ours, are like cockroaches in kitchens—not wanted, not encouraged but nevertheless they remain." Spending his life among them, he knew dancers and photographers too, as well as a few writers, though not many of these. He admired Gertrude Käsebier's fine things in photography and posed for her as early as 1907, at about the time when Albert Langdon Coburn took several photographs of Sloan and many of his paintings. Berenice Abbott was another photographer whom he greatly liked and admired later. As for writers, he had various clashes with Sadakichi Hartmann, the Japanese-German art critic who admired "The Cot," a painting of Sloan's that appealed to the literary mind, and he knew slightly Eugene O'Neill whom, with a number of others, he portrayed in the aquatint called "Hell Hole." † Another etching, "Frankie and Johnnie," was a note on the work of an author he liked, an episode from E. E. Cummings's play

* "I think that texture is one of the fundamental qualities of art—and I learned that lesson from the modern movement, the good cubist work of Picasso and Braque. Their pictures of guitar players and still lifes were exciting designs—major plastic wrinkles and interlocking shapes—clinched with graphic harsh textures—the big texture and the minor texture, lying on the surface within the picture plan, mysterious, living because imperfect."—Sloan, student notes.

† Another name for the "Tub,"—or "Bucket,"—"of Blood," the back room of a Sixth Avenue saloon, Wallace's, at the corner of West Fourth Street, where artists and writers gathered after the Brevoort closed for the night. O'Neill is the character in the upper right-hand corner of the picture.

*Him;** while Sloan was a friend of Edgar Lee Masters, who lived near him in the Hotel Chelsea where he was to live himself for sixteen years.

One village character whom Sloan knew was "Woe,"—Gertrude Drick Smith—a pupil whose visiting-card bore this pseudonym surrounded by the deepest mourning-band. She explained this by saying, "Woe is me." It was Woe who, in 1917, instigated the New Year's Eve party that Sloan commemorated in an etching when, with Marcel Duchamp and three friends of the stage, they climbed to the top of the Washington Arch over Stirling Calder's statue of the father of his country. Equipped with Chinese lanterns and toy balloons, they built a bonfire on the roof of the arch; then they read a proclamation that Greenwich Village was a new republic and declared its secession from the United States. They called on President Wilson to protect it as one of the small nations. Sloan named his etching "Arch Conspirators."

The door of the stairway of the arch was locked forever after.

* "*Him* is about as thrilling an evening's entertainment as I have ever experienced. I liked it thoroughly. I don't claim to understand it. I do not believe that a work of art can be or need be understood even by its maker. It seemed to me to be a glimpse inside the cranium of an artist-poet."—One of Sloan's notes, 1928.

## CHAPTER XIV

# THE LEAGUE: *GIST OF ART*

"I HAVE ALWAYS lived alone," John Sloan said once. "It is not in my nature to have many friends. I am too self-centred in my work." He was a maverick, as he often remarked, an estray even from the artist-herd, and lonelier than ever in his work after 1928 when he developed his later manner and felt he was largely ignored by the patron, the dealer, the critic and most students. During the twenties, moreover, he lost the two friends he had cared for most, J. B. Yeats and Robert Henri, while two others of the "Eight" died in the course of this decade. Maurice Prendergast was the first to go and Arthur B. Davies died in Florence, where he had been painting between visits to France to oversee the weaving of Gobelin tapestries after his own designs. Sloan had written to Miss Elizabeth Yeats in 1922: "That great man, your father, is no longer with us . . . The great warm glow has gone. A few score men such as your father in the world at any one time would cure its sickness . . . The church was full of his lovers, and they each felt as I did, that they had lost their father."

Sloan had once regarded Henri as a father too,—in art, —although they had gone separate ways in recent years; and, more than any other painter, Henri had always had the power to wound Sloan's heart and self-esteem. Sloan had hurt Henri as well, no doubt, in rejecting his methods and ideas, and this may perhaps have explained in part the silence of the older man when Sloan visited him in the hospital in his last illness. Sloan brought some of his new work to show his old master, and Henri looked at the pictures without saying a word. But it was Sloan who brought about the Henri memorial exhibition at the Metropolitan Museum in 1931, and he wrote the foreword for the catalogue. It made him happy to remember that Henri had said to Dolly once, "Take care of Sloan, for he is the best of us."

If Sloan was relatively solitary, he was so by his own wish, saying, with a touch of bravado, "I'm a lone wolf," and he often added, "I enjoy being disliked," for he was the most contrary of human beings. There was at times a streak of perversity in him when he took the opposite side in a discussion almost automatically and rejoiced that he made enemies thereby. On these occasions, he was "like a small boy on the Fourth of July running around with a torch," Helen Farr said; and the occasions often occurred at the Art Students' League, with which he had a sporadic but long connection. He had taught there fourteen years when, in 1931, he was elected president of the League, only to be defeated the following year when he remarked, "I am not running for the presidency. I will win it in a walk or not at all." With former prize students appointed as instructors and constantly perpetuating the methods and ideas they had acquired there, the school, he felt, suffered from inbreeding, and, believing it should search out new talents, he urged the appointment of George Grosz, who was leaving

Germany and Europe for the United States. He wanted Grosz because he was "a live example of academic training," a combination that he said was unknown in this country; but, regarding Grosz as a Bolshevik and trouble-maker, the board of control voted the appointment down. Sloan, virtually forced to resign, attacked the "art politicians" who were doing what no breeder of stock would do, following methods that would "kill stock of any kind." Ironically enough, two previous boards had invited George Grosz to teach at the League and he was employed a year later at the demand of the students; but after this incident three years passed before Sloan returned to the League and resumed his work there as a teacher.

Whatever were the rights and wrongs of the case, Sloan made "some pretty fine enemies" who were "not all in the graveyards" many years later,—some, even then, he said, had "not yet been admitted"; and he prided himself on their enmity, as he remarked in a speech at the time, because he well knew the reason for it. He was convinced that the men who opposed him were covered with the "pernicious spume of that poor dead thing in our cellar, the National Academy"; but the occasion showed him how many friends he had and how many felt that the League was dropping the pilot. He told one of his pupils that he felt "like an old battle-flag that has been shot full of holes in a good cause," adding, "but the flag still flies," while his pupils rallied about him and said they had taken him for granted too long, forgetting how much they owed him in their work. "The dead hand of the Academy," one or them said, "is out to capture the League and stop the flow of modern artists right at the source," and a large committee protested against the domination of a chauvinistic and politically biassed board. "The Art Students' League is Heartbreak House," another of the pupils remarked, where "high hopes for art and life" had been defeated,—the very life of "the flower of America" who came there every year "for artistic and for spiritual nourishment." Others who were later well-known painters expressed their devotion to Sloan himself in letters that must have touched him deeply, praising him for the impersonality with which he had played his part and for having always been for "the youth of today." *

Strong and courageous as Sloan was here, one might have thought him a little perverse in his feeling about George Grosz in after years, for he turned almost savagely against this fine artist for whom he had virtually staked his career at the League. Grosz himself wrote in his autobiography,

* "I for one never heard a direct slander at anyone from you . . . It may be a long while before we realize fully what you are doing and have done for so many hundreds, but I for one am grateful beyond measure . . . for you have divulged so much that has aided America to gain more art muscle."

"Your love for art, your fight for art, your keen interest in artists and everything that is vital and living is known to every thinking person. It is those fine elements in you that are feared by the Art Politicians, and for those very reasons they are your enemies."—Letters from Sloan's pupils.

At this time another well-known painter who said he had never met Sloan wrote to thank him for his "pioneering battle" on behalf of younger artists: "I want to take this opportunity of expressing to you my appreciation of the great things you have accomplished in art and for art in this country. I am one who is directly being benefited by your life and works . . . It is my hope that in my own work I may be able to achieve in part the power and artistic integrity so amply shown in yours."

*A Little Yes and a Big No,* that finding "a healthier and freer world" in this country, he ceased to see the evil he had seen at home, but Sloan, who realized why it was that the caricaturist had died in Grosz, was nevertheless unable to forgive him for it. He upbraided him for losing his gift for the "vitriolic attack." Nor could Grosz's admirers agree that this "great satirical draughtsman" had "degenerated into a sentimental German painter," producing "slimy nudes and skeletons standing in badly painted rubble for a public that thinks it is buying shocking art." But again, however this may have been, the affair of Sloan and Grosz at the League showed how far Sloan was from being chauvinistic, although he never showed any interest in travelling out of the United States and concentrated on the "American scene" so largely. It was because Grosz was a foreigner that Sloan suggested him for the League, to keep this from too much American inbreeding, saying that, as all painters used foreign canvas because it was the best, so they might profit also from foreign instructors. He felt that nationalism stood in the way of a broad human understanding, and he often said that outside pressure demanding the American scene had made him think twice before painting city-life subjects. Like all creative minds, he turned away instinctively from anything that was talked about too much, and he ridiculed the banality of the "American scene-painting" of factory-chimneys, scrap iron and rickety barns. Moreover, he liked to chasten his native country as "the great unspanked baby of the world." He said, "We are still a frontier society and we still have a frontier art," and that "American art is just a little bump in the Rocky Mountains of art history." He continued, "The discovery of America has done nothing yet for art," and he said that Columbus had wasted his time as compared with Hieronymus Bosch who discovered the "American scene" earlier than he. "America," said Sloan, "is the largest loudest brat the world has ever seen," but he had a strong feeling also that great art would spring up here when the country had "grown beyond the brat age."

But, to return to George Grosz, Sloan said he resembled this artist himself in being at his best "on the attack,"—meaning, in his own case, in public speaking,—and that just as Grosz was all right in Germany but "fell flat in a quieter environment," so it was with himself when he was on his feet. Once, at a meeting when he was asked to make a few remarks, he said, "I feel too friendly to be at my best," though it shocked him to discover that some of his students had been hurt by his "tabasco tongue" and felt that he had been more than unkind as a teacher. He had never intended his remarks to be entertained in a personal sense, and he thanked a poor memory for saving him from having to live with some of the things he had said about people and their work. How many of these were sarcastic, how many unjust! For behind his invective dwelt all the time a shy, sensitive, humble man with an innocent faith in mankind and a respect for his pupils that accompanied the respect he said they should feel for the model,* while, having what he called "cocktail courage," he had also much of the ordinary kind in the presence of what he considered corruption or

* "Be kind to human beings. Respect the model. Be very humble before that human being. Be filled with wonder at its reality and life."—*Gist of Art.*

Sloan's most condemnatory word was "heartless."

cheapness. Then the adrenalin flowed in his veins or the venom of the gadfly; and this occurred more and more as he advanced in life and became a public spokesman of the art-world.

Meanwhile, many of Sloan's opinions appeared in the book, *Gist of Art,* which was published in 1938, largely a collection of the impromptu remarks that he had delivered in class during the ten years preceding publication. The book, which Sloan put into final shape, had been organized by Helen Farr, who wrote a good part of it herself and who took regular notes of his talk and gathered other records contributed by his students and his friends. Already in 1935, Sloan had written to Helen Farr, "Your gentle but firm and wise personality is a great thing in my life," and, as a student, more than once, she took charge of his class at the League when for short periods he was obliged to be absent. Helen Farr had been studying with him since 1927. She found that many of the notes she collected were useless for publication because they meant something only in relation to the individual student's work, but Boardman Robinson was one of a number of artists who testified that the book was "superlatively" good as a manual for students.

Containing a large collection of plates of Sloan's work of every kind,—paintings, etchings, lithographs and drawings,—this book was a memorable array of the artist's perceptions, his technical and general knowledge and mother-wit. Occasionally truculent, sometimes wrong-headed,—as the outsider saw him,—Sloan usually appeared in these writings as singularly wise, while always abounding in his own sense as more and more a character, humorous, shrewd, magnanimous, high-principled and frank. So, and always more emphatically, he was to appear in the lectures and speeches he delivered at the League and elsewhere, over the radio or at Santa Fé, at the College Art Association, at dinners of the National Institute of Arts and Letters. His position at times was surprising when, "agin the government" as he was, he came out strongly, for example, on more than one occasion, for a government department of art, saying it would not be the right sort but it would be something to fight against and one would know where the enemy was to be found. Why honour the National Academy by according it this position? Sloan did not expect too much from a governmental department of art, for the French had had one for generations and our country could not be expected to do any better; and, with due respect for the antique, a government was sure to favour the commonplace in contemporary art. Sloan knew that a department of art would inevitably fall into the hands of the usual pernicious job-hunters and art-politicians, but he saw that the government's support of art during the depression made the country distinctly more "art-conscious." People who had supposed that "mural" was only a girl's name found it meant a picture in the post-office which they did not like; but at least they learned that there were such things as pictures. Sloan's final argument was that a Secretary of Art in the cabinet would give art in general a higher standing. Good art, he said, is the extreme tip of the tail of the art-kite, and, if the kite goes up, the tail will rise with it.

Always a rebel by temperament, Sloan had learned from Henri that art was a fight, along with life, and his constant bellicosity gave edge to many of his remarks, which were often semi-comic or semi-histrionic. He said people did not care enough about art now, they did not hate it enough and merely ignored it, and he suggested that one should work to get it sufficiently hated so that it would be prohibited altogether. This might result in our having "art-leggers," like the bootleggers of Prohibition, with perhaps an art-fleet twenty miles off shore and agents with rapid motor-boats dashing out at night. Then, if one went out to dinner, the host might press a button and a trap-door would open and reveal a picture. Would not all this make pictures highly exciting?—just as ordinary Prohibition led thousands of people, like Henri, to say, "Now it is every man's duty to have liquor in the house." Sloan felt that two years of art-prohibition would make us the most art-conscious of nations, and for this result he recommended a little "rough stuff" of the kind that had been used to get woman's suffrage. Meanwhile, governmental art-commissions reminded him of a cattle-ranch of the sort that he saw near Santa Fé, for the official authorities, he said, were all cattle-branders and in this respect they resembled the critics. For the critics too rounded up and branded artists, "according to the latest fashion of the Fogg Museum," and they "wanted their opinion to stick when they got you branded." For Sloan these "art-punchers" had the lingo and knew how to do their stuff, coralling the poor artists, throwing them and branding them Impressionists, Expressionists, Cubists and so on. Sloan said that on his tender flank he had been branded "Realist," which stood for the lowest grade of cow. Artists in the old days, he said, were like free cattle roaming the plains, free in all senses and free to starve, of course, but for Sloan even that freedom was worth while.

Like all vividly imaginative minds, Sloan hated labels and classifications, just as he hated conformity and standardization, and, as he had warned artists in earlier days to beware of the old "academy," so he warned them now against the "academy of modernism." It was a sad sight, he said, to see youth imitating men who in their day had been non-conformists, for had not the modernists grown out of a refusal to conform, creating a non-conforming system of production? And this was imitated now by artists who wished to conform and who were producing "cheap Picassos for the trade." The new "moderns," like the older ones, taking over the academies and juries, were still more intolerant of all variations, becoming themselves conservatives, corrupted by their power and forgetting all the lessons of growth and change. Far from repudiating modernism, Sloan had always continued to feel that it was a healthy return to the great principles of art, a cure for the sickness of the academic art that had tried to compete with the camera for three generations. That cubism was a good medicine he always insisted, for it led to an understanding, as he put it, of the plastic qualities of the old masters,—but he felt that in trying to escape from photography art was now trying to paint the unseen, in competition with psychoanalysis. Believing that non-objective art had lost much of the texture of life and that the modern experiments, healthy as they were, "must be absorbed into an art more human," he said that art needed "another vacation from art," a "new birth of humanism, a return to life." * He also said he did not think it was a sign of youth to feel that one *had* to follow the avant-garde of the moment, for "if you are doing what interests you perhaps it is the new thing that will be recognized later." The compulsion to conform greatly disturbed him, for it forced many young artists away from what they really wished to do, artists who would like to respond to the living world. How many put on Bosch-Breughel masks when they painted people for fear of being taken for illustrators, while artists, dealers and magazines frightened the public away from buying the sort of pictures they honestly liked. People were told that they had to "understand" art, and, as Sloan said, the only way to learn about art is to live with it, following one's taste and changing as one learns. Sloan felt that the art-world ought to be a "big swinging merry-go-round," with everyone following his own individual vision, "each artist on his own horse, riding for the fun of it," and, as Sloan put it, "reaching for the brass ring."

But, with all his strictures on the art of the time, Sloan never thought of looking back, or he looked back only to recall the flaccid art-world of his youth when Monet, with his satellites, loomed as the great planet. He could never have wished that time to return again, and his last word on the subject would always have been what he said once, "Art in America today is terrifically alive."

* Speaking of exhibitions of "modern art" in general, Sloan said in an interview in 1940 that they are "filled with test-tubes . . . These canvases are mostly like the retorts, crucibles and tubes in a laboratory where important experiments are going on. The workers are eagerly mixing every species of chemical in unheard-of combinations, in wild efforts to arrive at a new and effective product."

## CHAPTER XV

# SINAGUA

THE SLOANS HAD SETTLED in 1935 in the Hotel Chelsea, the picturesque caravansary in West Twenty-third Street where they were to spend their winters for the rest of their lives. It had "balcony accommodations for three hundred Juliets," John Sloan said, and the Pre-Raphaelite iron-work of the stairways and the balconies was supposed to have been designed by William Morris. There at various times O. Henry had lived, like William M. Chase in earlier years and the genius of the cinema, Robert Flaherty, later, and like Thomas Hart Benton, the painter, James T. Farrell and Thomas Wolfe, with Virgil Thomson and Carl Ruggles, the composers. The Chelsea was the temporary home of the Welsh poet Dylan Thomas at the time of his death in New York. For years it was the home as well of Edgar Lee Masters, who said the "damned pigeon-holers" obliged him to live in the shadow of the *Spoon River Anthology* and whose *Mitch Miller* Sloan illustrated in 1941. Sloan's contract with the publisher called for twenty-five drawings, but he became so interested in the story that he threw in twenty-five more.

Sloan himself soon felt at home in the high-ceilinged rooms of this old hotel, where the studio windows overlooked a great expanse of roofs, bringing back the summer nights of his first years in New York when he had watched the scenes in the opposite windows. He had felt that he saw there virtually all of humanity, which he recorded in the pictures that were now called "Sloans," the city pictures that seemed to him like another person's work, far from his present self both in time and in method. The critics who had called them "psychopathic" and "vulgar illustrations" now called them "romantic" or "nostalgic" or spoke of them as representing "romantic realism," two words that meant opposite qualities from Sloan's point of view. They had been painted in the days when the phrase "after Monet" stood for what "after Picasso" signified now, and it amused Sloan to think that he could make a living by selling this work he had done thirty years before. His reputation still rested on these city-life pictures, and the critics were always urging him to do them again, regarding him as a fool not to sit in his studio turning out new versions of "McSorley's Bar," the "Haymarket" and the "Wake of the Ferry." Just so, as editor of *Harper's Weekly,* Norman Hapgood had wanted him to do the kind of black-and-white work he had done for the *Masses,* and he could not make himself do for money what he had formerly, and so happily, done for nothing. "To repeat the other fellow's success or your own little success of the past,—that is a sign of old age," Sloan wrote. "We stay young by remaining students, experimenting." Besides, he was no longer the man he had been all those years ago and he had other fish to fry. He had no hope of paying the grocer by selling the work he was doing now, but the "fashion experts" had never meant anything to Sloan; and, for the rest, perhaps the future might think well of his present work as the present thought well of the work he had left behind him. He worked to please himself and a few understanding friends, and the moment he thought of painting from any other motive he found he could take no pleasure in his work at all.

While, as a man of sensibility, Sloan passed through many moods, he never knew a moment of self-pity, although he had no such provocation for it as one of the other veterans of the New York art-world. He had not been ignored like Louis Eilshemius, who called himself "the world's master artist" because others had scarcely admitted he was an artist at all,—the self-styled "Mahatma" who wrote to Sloan, "Why doesn't anybody come to see me instead of going to those stinkpot painters?" Sloan might have agreed with Eilshemius that "the great artist is *hidden* from the public" if he had felt that he himself was hidden, but his only grievance was that, after his varied productiveness,—his landscapes, portraits, life studies and what not,—he was still described as an "Ash-can" painter. However, saying to himself, "Oh, well!" he shrugged this off, tough-minded as he was and every day more absorbed in his work, "a student," as he said, "chewing on a bone." He felt more and more pervaded with a sense of ripeness. "I don't paint," he said, "from habit. Something gnaws at me, keeps me going," something that made it impossible for him to stay cooped up in the pigeon-hole where the critics felt they had safely tucked him away. Not that, in his own fashion, he was unwilling to turn out "Sloans," working to bring them, as he put it, "into graphic existence." He continued to paint a few city pictures, "Roofs in Chelsea," for example, "Roof

Chats" and "Fifth Avenue Critics," which was based on his old etching of 1905; but, on the whole, he had been weaned away from New York city life, in part by the automobiles that lined the streets. One could not see an incident or place because of the stream of cars rushing by. The subways were full of splendid material, but the people, as he said, moved out of the trains too quickly for him,—they were only good for abstract experiments,—and the women were ceasing to hang out their wash on the roofs and worked with electric machines in invisible cellars. Perhaps because his memory was not as keen as it had been, Sloan rarely saw city subjects that were good for him, much as he enjoyed Central Park on warm spring days. He liked to sit there on a bench and walk across the meadows with the Sunday pleasure-seekers and the lovers on the grass, when the lake was covered with experimental oarsmen and the girls were thicker than leaves on the ground in the autumn. He attempted a picture that he called "Central Park Landscape," with trees, a hill, rocks and the city beyond, but he had "no incentive," he said, to finish this.

In the Chelsea studio, however, he worked harder than ever,—interrupted on one occasion by the "modern child," *

* "To our apartment while we were thus engaged enters a sample of modern childhood, a little boy from the apartment next to ours. He is about four years old. He strolled in nonchalantly, looking around and over us. I felt we should be greeted in some way, so opened with 'Hello!' No response from the youngster. H. then greeted him. Still no response. I felt indignant at his rude disregard of us. We both repeated our 'Hello.' He looked at us with something of a mixture of disdain and disregard. I told him that one should greet folks on entering their house, etc. He stood with a baby smile on his face, his hand at his side slowly raised with a toy pistol drawn from his holster directed at me. He still said nothing and I sternly

—usually standing at his easel all day long till the light began to fade in the late afternoon. Sometimes he tried to sit at work in the old armchair he had used in the days of the Philadelphia *Press,* but he found that, unless he was doing a small detailed area, it was more tiring to work from a seated position. He usually had a pipe in his mouth, unlit as a rule, while he mulled over his pictures, often "stumbling,"—this might almost have been called Sloan's favourite word,—knowing that many of the pictures he was doing now might be more properly called experiments or studies. He had never fabricated city pictures and he could and would not do so; besides, he believed that nowadays he was putting more into his work and he felt the need of models to get fullness in the forms. Persuaded that his work was very uneven, he was convinced as well that some of it was more powerful and truly creative than any of the pictures he had painted as a younger man;* and he spent a good deal of time in the "tinkering department," as he called it, the "repaint and editing department" of "revisions and corrections." He reworked some of his older pictures in which the proportions were exaggerated or there were certain areas that seemed to him dead, and sometimes the drawing of the drapery was

---

ordered him out of the place. He left slowly and defiantly . . . Sample of the youth who are to manage the world of the future."—One of Sloan's notes.

* At one point in his notes Sloan said, "The big nude standing at the foot of the stairs I feel is the zenith of my work." But elsewhere he expressed doubts regarding this, saying that for certain textural reasons he had included too much pubic hair. Because of this, he felt, it would "never be a great painting . . . Titian never noticed the pubic hair, and most of the other great figure painters omitted that human decoration."

too casual, he felt.* In his picture of the auction-room he changed the figures in the front, painting out a space with tempera, and he amended "McSorley's at Home," making the wall cooler, lightening the floor and changing to a light grey the coat of the central figure. "McSorley's Saturday Night" was another picture that was greatly improved in this way by after-thoughts. Ten years after it had left his hands he saw this old picture afresh and made an important change in the composition, something few people would notice but essential, he felt, to the quality of the light and the clarity of the design. There were too many little angles disturbing the general plan and too many hats accented with lines and outlines. He was bent on "ironing out" casual factors, at the same time eliminating small truths he had observed that cluttered the large order of the whole. Sloan also reworked his "Nude Girl on a Green Sofa," painting the pillow yellow and changing the surroundings. Thinking of Isadora Duncan, following the big movements of the music while she ignored the lesser ornamentation, Sloan kept his eye steadily on the main rhythms of his theme.

Meanwhile, he spent many evenings poring over plates, usually in colour, of Fouquet, Signorelli, Rubens, Giovanni Bellini, and he said he liked to have a book of Donatello's work around, for his bas-reliefs were so full of significant drawing. Mantegna's "Dead Christ" was a picture he never tired of studying, deeply involved as he was in the problem of perspective,—he had a reproduction of it with him all the time and he saw in it more with every look. The force of the

* Apropos of this he said, "A plain grey shawl is more difficult to paint than an embroidered or damask drapery."

signs of projection and recession was such that the picture, he said, literally pushed the observer away from the canvas until he was able to see it from the proper distance. Sometimes regretting what he called his own "false start," Sloan became engrossed in the study of the masters of the past, and it pleased him to think that Giotto, Bosch and a score of other ancestors had been, as he put it, restored to leadership. Hearing of friends who were going to Italy, he envied them at times for seeing, for instance, Piero della Francesca, while more and more he recorded his impressions after visiting the Metropolitan Museum, the Brooklyn Museum or perhaps the Frick collection. In the latter he delighted in the great Rembrandts and in Gainsborough's picture of St. James's Park. He dwelt on the solidity of the drawings of Ingres and the magic in the modelling of a certain Memling portrait he had seen, or the inscrutable beauty of a Roger van der Weyden, the portrait of a woman with a white kerchief. "A very great piece of painting," this, "sculptural, a lovely thing, infinitely subtle in colour and form"; and how, in the wonderful "Venus and Mars," had Paolo Veronese contrived to keep light the painting of the flesh in shadow? He exclaimed over the character of the forms in a Van Ostade drawing that was "monumental in design without being dramatic . . . just common people in a scene of daily life," and a Breughel in which geometric lines led the eye from group to group, at one point passing across an empty space. Sloan was keenly interested in the exhibition of Hogarth, Constable and Turner at the Metropolitan Museum in 1947, struck by Constable's love for the things he was painting, "his ground so solid and his forms so felt." Beside Constable, it seemed to him that Turner was thin and artificial in spite of his later "fine emotional painting." Constable, too, had lived at a time that needed, as he said, a "jar . . . against literary tight academic work."

While, no doubt, Sloan spent more hours over books and colour prints than he spent in galleries and museums, he missed few important exhibitions in his later years, and he was deeply interested in the great show of French tapestries that also took place at the Metropolitan Museum. He was able to study at close range their technique and their colour. On another occasion, it struck him that Copley, "monumentally clumsy" as he was, might have been the Giotto of an American Renaissance, an artist beside whom Albert Ryder, Sloan came to feel, was "just a minor poet whistling in the dark." But, thinking of the older masters, he always went back to Carpaccio and his nobility of mass, proportion and design, how full, how controlled, how simple and yet how ample! In these studies he found some of his old values changing. After one exciting visit to the Metropolitan Museum he wrote, "Discovered how Hals fades in presence of the great ones," and elsewhere he remarked in one of his notes, "Daumier can hardly be called an important painter." He still persisted in his belief that, in line drawing, John Leech remained "the peer of any of the greatest masters"; but he said, "My old gods Manet, Hals, Velasquez no longer have much weight with me,—now that I admire the Italian primitives, Carpaccio, Signorelli, etc. You can't succeed very well in imitating those giants."

On their way to and from Santa Fé, the Sloans stopped every spring and fall for a visit at the Art Institute in Chicago to see the great El Greco and the Picassos; and Sloan wished that the New Mexico Museum had a few pictures that required guards instead of being a "little pond for tadpoles." You could choose a time around three o'clock, drift in looking like an artist and take anything out under your arm, and you could even back up a truck and move a piece of sculpture out of the door and no one would stop you. When someone remarked that this museum was "full of life," Sloan said there was plenty of life under stones in the woods, creeping and squirming in a small world of its own that was not unlike the world of the Santa Fé artists. For they had no contact with the great world of the past. Santa Fé was a Mount Ararat and everything reached it a little late, while, instead of having a permanent collection of really fine things, the museum was little better than a bazaar for tourists. Any artist could exhibit there and the result was that pot-boiler artists used the museum and sat around selling their work. Its unwritten policy was to obtain only work of the Southwest, and for this reason it had refused Witter Bynner's great collection of Chinese paintings and jades, objects that Bynner wished to leave there, along with his Indian collection, for the study of cultural relationships between the Indians and the Chinese. How this would have widened the horizon of the local artists! But many years were to pass before the museum, altering its policy, acquired these remarkable collections. Thanks to the New Mexico Art Alliance, established in 1949, there were some changes for the better in this museum, which had also encouraged low standards in the craft-work of the Indians until it began to "screen" this at the same moment. The time was coming when, to Sloan's delight, the best pueblo artists were proud of sending their finest things to be shown there and when they told tourists to "see my real work in the museum."

In all this, Sloan revealed the great change in his own point of view when he had come to see eye to eye with Renoir, who replied to Meier-Graefe's question *where* a young man became an artist, "In the museum, *parbleu!*" To Sloan it was sad that this great community of artists should have had one of the weakest museums in the country, and largely owing to the "open door" policy,—"let them all in," —that ended by merely encouraging sales to tourists. This too was the result of Henri's teaching and his influence over the founder when, in 1917, visiting Santa Fé, he had fallen in with Dr. Edgar Hewett,—the very same open door policy Sloan advocated in New York, the policy of the Society of Independent Artists. But he saw that what was good for an exhibition might not be good for a museum.

Sloan, for the rest, had been glad to use one of the studios which the museum provided for visiting artists,—he had done much work there in 1919,—and he never lost interest in the museum. It was at his suggestion in 1946 that a travelling exhibit of Indian paintings and drawings went the rounds of a number of Southwestern pueblos. Sloan hoped that this imaginative approach to the treatment of the pueblo life might excite more of the Indian artists to replace with finer work their routine stylized and poster-like manner. He regretted that he himself had not in earlier days collected Indian paintings instead of rugs, and he continued to write interpretations of Indian art, collaborating on one occasion with Oliver LaFarge.* In 1946 he wrote an introduction to Ira Moskowitz's *Indian Pattern and Ceremonials,* a book for which John Collier provided the text. For his drawings Ira Moskowitz had selected incidents of Indian life that had impressed him personally, and Sloan had been struck by the difference between this work and the work of previous illustrators and artists. It was truer than the old pictorial approach of the European and American mind to the representation of Indian life and customs, with its pseudo-classical athletes and bacchantes, for Moskowitz had regarded the Indians not with preconceived ideas but with friendliness, respect and even awe. He had recorded the feelings of a sympathetic fellow-man in the presence of a culture that was ages older than his own, and he understood the great ritual dances, invocations to rain and corn, that had long fascinated Sloan.

Retaining their old house in the Calle Garcia, the Sloans, in 1941, built another six miles out of town, an adobe dwelling on a hill, with a fine view of the Santa Fé landscape, which they called Sinagua,—"without water." It was furnished with tables and chairs with Indian designs and with Navajo, Hopi, and Mexican rugs, red, orange, gold, black and blue as well as the natural white, grey and brown. Against the pine floors and white walls these were rich in colour. There were certain Gloucester marines among the paintings, and the Sloans were entertained at meals by the

* Sloan also read for possible errors regarding the technique of painting the manuscript of LaFarge's novel *The Copper Pot,* about artist life in New Orleans.

out-of-doors animal comedy of finches, lizards, horned toads, rabbits and chipmunks. They once saw a catamount strolling near the crest of the hill. Every day there was a sabbath where nothing broke the stillness but the calls of the birds and the hum of insects, and Sloan rejoiced in the great skies and the clean dry air, always a relief after the New York winter. There he had time, with his painting, for reading and music, for Boswell's Johnson, a "great book," Boccaccio whom he read again, and Plutarch's Lives which he said never grew stale. These lives reminded him that social problems had not changed very much. Either at Sinagua or in New York he read new translations of the Iliad and the Odyssey and he found *Tristram Shandy* "such a wonderful book" that he could scarcely bear to put it down, so "tender" it was, with "such a gracious humour." This humour, he said, had "a clean mind behind it," while he was moved by Edith Hamilton's *The Greek Way* and *The Roman Way* as well as by Knut Hamsun's *The Growth of the Soil.* He was stirred by Burckhardt's prophecy of the coming totalitarian age and in other ways by Richard Wright's *Black Boy* and Carson McCullers' *The Heart Is a Lonely Hunter,* along with Sinclair Lewis's *Cass Timberlane,* the work of a "grim, stern, sympathetic artist." Sloan remarked that "a good novel gives one an opportunity for experience that does not present itself in actual life." At the same time, Thomas Craven's *Men of Art* pleased him by the stress it laid on the humanity and strength of great artists. Almost every night he played Victrola records, preferring music with a strongly marked form like Bach's chorales and early church music, although he was also particularly fond of Brahms. Otherwise he chose mountain ballads, salty rough popular story-telling music and Negro records, so human yet so close to the jungle. This was the kind of music he liked when he was painting, saying that it was an insult to great artists to use their work as "background" while one's mind was busy with something else.

One of the reasons that Sloan loved Santa Fé, he said, was that you heard the Mexicans singing there or playing their own music on their cheap little phonographs, especially on the Canyon Road at night. Willa Cather had also delighted in this, and, although his friend Edgar Varèse rebuked him, saying the music was all sentimental, Sloan loved these Mexican things, half sung, half spoken. Meanwhile, in Santa Fé, he saw a good deal of Randall Davey and other friends, most of them artists or writers, with Miss Amelia Elizabeth White, to whom so many owed so much, and Mrs. Cyrus McCormick, that other benefactor. There was Witter Bynner, with what Sloan called "a romantic house in a romantic garden," and another old friend Will Shuster, the Philadelphia artist, who lived in the foothills to the west of the town and whose house-warming Sloan had commemorated in his painting "The New Homestead" in 1930. The two carried on, as Sloan put it, a "duel in paint," reciprocally painting one another's portraits, and one day Witter Bynner joined the Sloans for lunch at Shuster's and brought along his translation of Lao-tse. Sloan felt, as he listened, that, if it were applied, the wisdom of this Chinese sage might well solve the frightful situation of the world of our day.

## CHAPTER XVI

# NEW BEGINNINGS

One day a station-wagon drew up at the door of the Chelsea and several men got out with cameras in their hands. They had come to take moving-picture records of John Sloan in his studio and to carry him off later for a drive through the city. They wanted "shots" of the scenes of his old paintings for an "educational news profile" of Sloan, who was driven to the Lafayette and the arch in Washington Square, to the Garibaldi statue and a bend in the Elevated railway. At the end he was taken to Cortlandt Street for a reminiscent picture of the "Wake of the Ferry," but not before he had stopped at the Hotel Judson, where he had had a studio for nearly nine years. Spacious, with a ceiling twenty feet high and many spots for posing the model, and with its outlook over the animated square, this had been John Sloan's favourite studio; but, although he had offered to teach there in order to keep it, the expanding New York University had cast him out.

For Sloan this drive in the moving-picture van was a "retrospective" in real life, and so was the return of the native when, at the age of sixty-five, he had gone back to Lock Haven, where he was born. He had been visited some years before by a cousin, John Sloan Dickey, soon to become the president of Dartmouth College, another native of this town who told him how famous he was there and urged him to return for a glimpse of the place.* A reception committee met him at the station and Sloan had been surprised to find how beautiful was this corner of Pennsylvania, especially the view from the graveyard where his forbears lay buried, overlooking the Susquehanna and the hills beyond. He spoke at a large public meeting attended by crowds from neighbouring towns,—a few travelled a hundred miles to see him; and he talked with the young people who were interested in art and who came to the exhibition of his paintings and etchings. Meanwhile, beginning in 1938 at the Addison Gallery in Andover, there were regular retrospectives of John Sloan's work, at Wanamaker's in New York, at the Renaissance Society in Chicago, at Dartmouth College, Kraushaar's and the Hudson Guild. In 1941, at Petitpas', a dinner was given for Sloan by the Society of Independent Artists. Frank Crowninshield was the toastmaster and among the speakers were Oliver LaFarge, Henry Schnakenberg, Juliana Force and the author of this book. By that time Sloan was represented in collections in Capetown and Singapore, Calcutta and Shanghai as well as Australia and Europe.†

* Oddly, enough, at about this time, Sloan became aware of another John Sloan who was presumably a distant cousin. Belonging to an older generation, this other John Sloan was also an artist whose pictures began to turn up during these years. It was known that at some time he had studied in Paris.

† Three monographs on Sloan were published during his lifetime. One was by A. E. Gallatin, another by Guy Pène du Bois and the third was the first in the "American Artists" series. Lloyd Goodrich's illustrated study of Sloan was published by the Whitney Museum in 1952, the year after his death.

Sloan had come to be variously described as the "dean of American artists," the "undefeatable liberator" and the "old war-horse," and the former "apostle of ugliness" was now called the "old master." He was accustomed to letters of praise such as Lee Simonson wrote him, saying, "What a real person you are!"; but, when someone used the epithet "great," he doubted if he could live up to this,—"or perhaps greatness isn't much from the inside point of view." He said he had had so much publicity that he would have been a millionaire if he had been a manufacturer, whereas even at seventy he could scarcely pay the doctor from the proceeds of his own proper work. People did not like, he said, "what I am doing now," but what he was "doing now" they never had liked, although a few eccentric people had enjoyed his city work when it was done, as a few eccentrics enjoyed his later pictures. One sort of critic complained that he had been influenced by the Armory Show, another sort complained that he had not been, but he was disturbed when younger people turned away from what he was doing while they were excited by his "old grey and brown" work. Witter Bynner in Santa Fé had urged him in a long serious talk to go back to painting scenes and people instead of doing so many figure pictures,—to return to the day when he was the "American Hogarth,"—and he sometimes lay awake at night wondering if he had gone out on a limb with this technical problem of underpainting and glazing. Were these critics right? he asked himself. "Have I wasted my efforts of the last twenty-five years? Am I leaving emotion out of this later work?" But he always ended by saying, "I cannot believe it."

It would not have been so difficult to sit back and try to

re-create what he had done forty years before. He could probably have recovered the mood of these earlier things, and this was what Everett Shinn was doing, painting clowns and vaudeville scenes because he had a dealer who could sell them.* But it did not interest Sloan merely to echo his old self, even if the struggle to create was a real struggle after one reached threescore years and ten; and Walter Pach was not the only critic he respected who were sure he was doing "by far" his finest work. Pach felt that his city pictures were only his "genre period" and that his later work was not only more important but belonged to a more important class of art, and Henry McBride enthusiastically supported this opinion. So did Forbes Watson who said that Sloan, unlike so many of his contemporaries who had seen their success vanish, was never "out," and he might have added that this was because Sloan had "character," the character that is so much rarer than "talent." Always a favourite of literary men, Sloan must have been pleased by a letter he received in 1939 from the poet and critic John Gould Fletcher, saying he had begun to understand the later style that placed Sloan among the "great plastic painters." †

* "What a paradox that we two should be the last of the 'Eight,' Shinn . . . catching up with the demand for pictures by the 'Eight' who were rejected in their day."—One of Sloan's notes. William J. Glackens, Sloan's friend from boyhood, had died in 1938 after visiting him in a hospital a day or two before.

† "I feel I owe you a letter. I was yesterday only a passer-by going by your studio. Now I know and understand you better . . . You have moved from the surface-sensation of the impressionists to the form-sensation of the great plastic painters . . . To eyes used to your earlier method, the later comes as a shock, but you are the greater painter for having taken all this up, and more likely to achieve a secure place in the American art of the future . . . Look back—a

Suddenly, at a moment when Sloan himself had been gravely ill, Dolly died one morning of a heart-attack. A hundred times she had visited palmists to learn when Sloan was going to die, fearing that she could not exist in the world alone, and now Sloan was obliged to travel without her, weak as he was, to Santa Fé, after having undergone several operations. He had had, he said, six major surgical adventures, the result of a sadly inadequate digestive system, so many operations, in fact, that he added in a note, "The next time they will have to put in a zipper." This had led him into all manner of experiments with diet against which J. B. Yeats had long since warned him, and his illness coincided with feelings of depression and a consciousness that perhaps he was losing his grip. There were days when he was idle, cross and gloomy, when he seemed to have less proficiency with each canvas, when he had to fight his way with every picture he undertook and he felt bereft of the verve and assurance of youth. It was as if he had been drained, as if all the life in him sank through his feet and spread out on the floor like a rug, and he was disgusted with his work and convinced that perhaps for fifteen years everything he had done had been a failure. On the other hand, it had always been a bad sign with him when he thought the work was

man of your age cannot help looking back—but never *turn back!* Rembrandt was the greatest painter of all time because he could not turn back; and the last Rembrandts are the greatest because in them were fused his final knowledge of form and his final verdict on life. I think I see something of that sort coming along in you and your very latest work. I believe that America has every right to be proud of you as a painter. I say this because I feel I know by some instinct (maybe a poet's instinct) what painting amounts to."—John Gould Fletcher to John Sloan.

going too well, whereas if it was really going right he began to feel faint and actually wanted to stop, at least for a while. The truth was that, in spite of his weakness, in spite of the critics and in spite of his doubts,—slowly as he worked nowadays,—Sloan was not to be downed for years to come. He was even, in his seventies, to blossom out with brilliant crimsons, purples and blues, colours he had scarcely used before.

Good fortune, moreover, awaited him in 1944, a year after Dolly's death, when he remarried, when Helen Farr joined him in Santa Fé and he was able to write before long, "We are happy enough in one year to fill three." Helen Farr had been teaching art at the Nightingale-Bamford school in New York and doing art-therapy work for doctors there; and this opened what he was to call a "beautiful period in my life" that made every anniversary a "day of thanksgiving." He was to write on the seventh anniversary, "What a thankful and happy man I am that this happened to me!", for Helen had surrounded him with a gay and healthy atmosphere, not "stirring him up," like Dolly, but "calming him down." Together they painted every day and Helen prepared for exhibitions of her work at Santa Barbara and San Francisco, while he painted her in a green hat, in a red dress, in a blue striped blouse, in "The Necklace," in the picture that he called "Tea for One." It was a pleasure for Sloan to see the little green piñon trees merrily clad in the wash drying in the wind on quiet days when a great sun-drenched world of wooded hills and mountains stretched all about them as far as the eye could reach. They wandered and basked outside the house like Adam and Eve in the garden, sun-bathing among the dwarf cedars and juniper trees, forgetting that twenty-five miles away there were atom-bombs at Los Alamos, supposedly powerful enough to wreck the planet. Sometimes Sloan strolled about in shorts tearing the parasite growths, with tentacles like seaweed, off the piñons, the little trees that stood, as he wrote, still and thankful on summer days, with damp thrills through their roots, whenever it rained. Young in heart, in the senses, in the mind, Sloan woke up every morning with a fresh radiant interest in the new day, and, as Helen wrote later, he and she worked and played together as if their days were never to have an end.

It was true, as Sloan said, that, at threescore and ten, time passed "like an avalanche," but, largely thanks to his habit of work, with his courage and his patience, his good health had come back, as it appeared, to stay. He seemed to have regained all his old vigour, and in this wonderful Santa Fé climate he could stand an amazing amount of work, rebounding quickly from fatigue. If he worked with difficulty, one of the reasons was that he never followed a formula in anything he did,—whatever he undertook was a fresh creation,—and he worked with such intensity that Helen induced him to vary the day with carpentry or possibly painting the eaves of the house. He had started to write an elaborate diary again in 1948, and he plastered holes in the adobe walls to keep out the chipmunks and wild mice and sometimes made costumes for the Fiesta. Once he made costumes,—"gasoline pumps,"—for the Hysterical parade, the travesty of the somewhat dull Historical parade that was an annual event in Santa Fé. Sloan still enjoyed clowning, as of old, quoting Leo Stein's remark, "There is nothing like growing old without dignity"; for, as he said, this preserves one's self-respect even if perhaps one loses the respect of others. Helen had made costumes and scenery for the King-Coit school plays in New York, and once at a party at Miss White's Sloan made a hit in a creation of hers, a vermilion "Botticelli" costume with a black wig. He might have passed for Lorenzo de' Medici in this. It was Helen who started the New Mexico Alliance for the Arts to stimulate cultural activities in Santa Fé, as Dolly had worked for the recognition of the Indian arts.

Sloan, however, had less interest in community affairs, and, after working, he usually preferred a walk, perhaps with the kitten that Helen had given him and that he loved to watch, so independent it was and so beautiful in movement. The "wonder cat" Dobie sometimes followed him for miles, occasionally stopping to climb a piñon tree. Sloan enjoyed watching all animals, beginning with the pigeons whom he studied through his field-glasses from the window in New York, redrawing, after years of observation, the flying birds in his "Roofs in Chelsea," fascinated as he was by their patterns of flight. He had had an aquarium for a while and a pet toad brought from Gloucester which he had studied by the hour, observing that, accustomed as it was to flies, it had trouble digesting chopped meat, so that now and then Sloan had to massage its belly. He also had a small water-turtle, but this became a nuisance, constantly getting lost behind a box or a trunk; while he delighted in a pet white rat that liked to nibble spaghetti sticks and greatly enjoyed nips of whiskey and water. It ran about freely but was glad to return to its cage. Sloan once said that he hated people who had dogs as pets because they always kept them in a state of dependence, as undignified for an animal as it was for a man, but this fiery libertarian seemed to have no such objection when it came to the lesser breeds of the animal kingdom. He sometimes went to the zoological gardens in New York, remarking that the owls were his "favourites," so dignified they were, and there he stood and looked at the buffaloes, on more than one occasion, for hours at a time. It astonished him to realize that many of the Indians in Santa Fé who performed the Buffalo Dance had never seen one.

Often, there in Santa Fé, the Sloans drove out in the afternoon, perhaps to some spot along the Rio Grande where Sloan made a tempera sketch and Helen a painting, delighting in the great dark formations near the red-running river with gleaming ribbons of blue reflected from the sky. They drove to the church at Abiquia or stopped for hours painting in the lovely silence of the old ghost town of Cerillos. Occasionally they had to drive for miles to find a subject that suited Sloan, while at other times he would say, "Put me down anywhere." He liked this gravel-washed landscape dotted with intense greens, while he always felt humble in the presence of the age-old hills, thrust up from the earth and invariably noble. He disliked the local landscape-painting with mountains that looked like plaster of Paris splattered, as he put it, with a "stuttering air-brush," by little-god artists with no feeling for the mystery of nature. These artists were devoid of respect for the grandeur of mountains that had been there for millions of years before men existed, and for him their work was "an indignity, an insult." He would have agreed with Leo Stein that New Mexico was one of the tremendous things, recalling the vision of the great Chinese landscape painters. Sloan, painting, tried to understand the "sculptural entity" of the scene, analyzing the colour he saw into the prevailing undercolours on which the textural incidents occurred.

But, much as he enjoyed landscape painting, for Sloan the human element was always more engrossing than any other, and, just as he had said that "life" meant more to him than "art," so he cared more for "people" than he cared for "scenes." All this continued to be true even in the years since the Armory Show and after he had become "serious" about his work,—"aware," at last, as he said, "of the technique of art," for which he cared almost as much as Ingres, who copied a Holbein at eighty or more, "so as to learn," he remarked to a friend. The last book Sloan illustrated was *Of Human Bondage,* by Somerset Maugham, for which he made sixteen etchings in 1937, etchings that pleased the author so much that he planned to use them to decorate his new house in South Carolina. For they had "caught wonderfully the tang of the period," said Maugham, and made readers "eager to know more about the people," communicating Sloan's own fertilizing sense of the interest and joy of existence, his love of humankind, his liberality and zest. One of his amusements was to find odd forms in the covers of popular magazines, the *Saturday Evening Post, Collier's* or *Life,* and with a few touches of crayon and scrapings with the pen-knife expose the absurdities in these commercial drawings. For his interest in life and humanity was unflagging to the end, and it was notable that in 1948, painting the Plaza in Santa Fé, he was most concerned with "populating" the panel. Several times he returned to the scene of the old Civil War monument to wait for some human incident that would "complete the picture as far as motive was concerned," sitting there again and again watching the passers-by before he found the right figures to provide his incentive.

But Sloan cared nothing for "realism" that was not "realization," and he had no use for the photographic representational art that was rightly condemned, he felt, by the abstract artists. Once, at a semi-public dinner, he found himself seated side by side with a well-known young painter whose great popular success was based on this kind of work that he disliked and regarding whom he said in his diary, "He's all right personally—they always are" but to whom he presently spoke with his usual candour. He told the young man that he should try working with his left hand to impede the fatal facility with which he painted and that he should study Carpaccio and other great artists who had always drawn from "memory concepts." This was at a time when Sloan was a spokesman of the art-world, always ready to speak wittily and well,* finding that when he rose to his feet all manner of thoughts rushed into his mind that had never even remotely occurred to him before. He paid tribute to Johann Pogozeba, the Polish refugee landscape painter, at the opening of the "Hell's Kitchen Art Galleries" on Tenth Avenue in New York, and he joined Niles Spencer, Edgar Varèse, Holgar Cahill and Stuart Davis at a Bleecker Street

* Apropos of this he remarked in his diary, "Any man who speaks English with care is suspected of being a fairy nowadays."

dinner in honour of Romany Marie. This "old-time provider of philosophy and food" looked, "in her happiness," he wrote, "fine and handsome." Then, with Bishop Manning and Carl Van Doren, he proposed the establishing in Washington Square of a "living art centre" for painters, sculptors and writers in the row where Frank Norris and O. Henry had lived, with Willa Cather, Eugene O'Neill, E. A. Robinson, Stephen Crane and Theodore Dreiser.

This was at about the time when, in 1950, the gold medal of the National Institute of Arts and Letters was conferred on the thorny refractory doubting artist who felt that awards were never given to the best. Sloan had always been sure that honours were bad for young artists, though perhaps he was so old they could do him no harm, convinced as he still was that, if other artists liked his work, he needed no other proof that it could not be good. Considering, however, that as most of the members of the Institute were not artists, that about three-quarters of them were composers or writers, he was reconciled to receiving this award,—on the understanding that it was a tribute not to his art but to his independence.

CHAPTER XVII

# TERMINUS

JOHN SLOAN had always supposed that he had a blacksmith's heart, but this proved not to be the case, and the time came in 1951 when his doctor told him that he could not return to Santa Fé. The altitude there would be a strain for him, so Helen cast about for another retreat for the summer months where he might find good subjects and people whom he liked. He was not altogether sorry to give up Santa Fé, where he felt he was treated as a character, as an old man, and where his age seemed to be of more interest than his painting, as if he was "an elderly spider at work on a web." Then one day in the late spring the Sloans visited friends in Connecticut, where Sloan was impressed by the great "civilized" trees and hills, and Helen remembered how this change of scene had swept away his prejudice against the summer green world of the East. The country had struck him as delightfully strange and new, and Helen, reminding him of this, suggested that they might try a summer at Hanover, New Hampshire. There John Sloan Dickey was now president of Dartmouth College and the great Orozco murals were in the library there.

The experiment was a complete success, for Sloan, already in his eightieth year, adapted himself almost at once to these novel surroundings. He had all the elasticity of a man in his thirties, although he was frightened a little at first by the blinding green of the countryside, amazed as he also was by its bewildering wetness. After thirty-two summers in the Southwest, he felt, as he said, "like a desert scorpion dropped in a green salad." But he presently discovered, north of the college, a spot that made him feel at home, a wooded area with tall trees and large granite rocks with cave-like clefts. This "Bema," the college assembly green, acted on his mind at once and turned his "point of view," Helen said, "outward," changing his mood to a positive one and serving as the spark that set his motor going, even at first "racing." But he soon arrived at the right rhythm, and when, on August 2nd, his eightieth birthday occurred, he had wholly ceased to regret Santa Fé. He had taken over Hanover, as Helen put it, and, pleased with the old farmhouses and barns, he was back at his normal system of working and "grousing" at himself. He studied the elm-trees, charmed by the rolling and tossing country, hills alternating with dales, "green, greener, greenest," and he was soon painting the Vermont and New Hampshire pasture-land, "struggling," he said, "with the cows."

Only a few months before, Lloyd Goodrich had come to the Chelsea to select Sloan's pictures for the Whitney Museum show, the great retrospective exhibition of the following winter that revealed the surprising variety and extent of his work. Sloan was not to see this, although he had waked on his eightieth birthday with the triumphant feeling, "There, I've made it!" and although, at Hanover, he had been at the top of his form, planning to build a studio and buy a house there. He was happy in New Hampshire, and when the art department of the college bought his nude Negro girl he said, "I knew then that Dartmouth was a liberal college." Dartmouth had also acquired "Roofs in Chelsea" and "McSorley's Back Room," together with a group of Sloan's drawings and prints and a complete file of the *Masses*. The Orozco murals had struck Sloan at once as uncluttered by the multitude of symbols and objects that made most murals, he remarked, "like patches of wall-paper glued together"; and he was expecting to spend summers there for many years to come, feeling he would need them all to paint this scene. He could not regard his new landscapes as properly finished. But, like Titian, Ingres and Renoir, he was opening his ninth decade with a consciousness that he was at his best, and he understood what Maxfield Parrish meant in a remark one afternoon, "When we reach our age we should live as if we had thirty years to live." He had not seen this artist, with whom he had little in common, since they had been students in Philadelphia, when, working together at the Academy, they had met again at some of the plays at 806 Walnut Street. Professor Herbert F. West soon became a friend of Sloan, and all the more naturally because he was writing a study of Voltaire and other sympathetic rebels; and one day the Sloans called on the author of *The Lost Weekend,* Charles Jackson, who lived at Orford, not far away. Then Robert Frost suddenly appeared one afternoon, greeting Sloan with the words, "I came to admire."

But this was at the hospital, where Sloan found himself one day after a good morning of work painting the "Red

Silo," even working after lunch putting a white triangle on the forehead of the cow in the foreground. The day before he had made a sketch of the studio he was intending to build on a spot that he and Helen had carefully chosen, and he had six pictures under way; but he had become philosophic, he said, and he only objected to operations because they broke in upon his work. He had learned to "let himself go and float along like a leaf on the stream, gently, gently," his words of counsel to another patient who was also to undergo an operation. He began to read Lamb's *Essays of Elia,* "not for the first time," he noted in the diary he continued to write, remarking, "While the light of old age flickers low in thc socket, the flames of youth are brightly crackling." For his hospital room was in the children's section. He said, going in to the operation, "Take good care of my cane," the walking-stick he had cut in the woods of New Hampshire, adding, to Helen, "It's a fight, isn't it?" expressing in this last phrase the feeling that had governed him all through life. Referring to Helen, he had said in his diary, "We share a bright hope," but he had had too many operations; and so passed this good man, fearless, truthful, innocent and wise, who had always lived in a world that knew no time.

# INDEX